BERLIN

MINI MAP+GUIDE

CONTENTS

EXPERIENCE

NEED TO KNOW

Left: The Mitte district divided by the Spree
Right: Inside the Reichstag dome

KEY TO MAIN ICONS

- Map
- Address/Location
- Telephone
- Train
- S-Bahn
- U-Bahn
- Tram
- Bus
- Visitor information
- Open
- Closed
- Website

PRICE GUIDE

Throughout the guide the following price categories have been applied:

€€€ On a budget €€€ Mid-range
€€€ Splurge

A NOTE FROM DK TRAVEL

The rate at which the world is changing is constantly keeping the DK travel team on our toes. While we've worked hard to ensure that this edition of Berlin is accurate and up-to-date, we know that opening hours alter, standards shift, prices fluctuate, places close and new ones pop up in their stead. So, if you notice we've got something wrong or left something out, we want to hear about it. Please get in touch at travelguides@dk.com

Main Contributors Petra Falkenberg, Alexander Rennie

Design Divyanshi Shreyaskar, Priyanka Thakur, Stuti Tiwari

Editorial Dharini Ganesh, Sarah Mathew, Beverly Smart

Picture Research Virien Chopra, Vagisha Pushp, Nishwan Rasool

Cartography Suresh Kumar

Pre-production Rajdeep Singh, Tanveer Zaidi

Production Controller Kariss Ainsworth

Art Director Maxine Pedliham

Publishing Director Georgina Dee

Content previously published in DK Berlin (2025).
This abridged edition first published in 2020

Published in Great Britain by Dorling Kindersley Limited
DK, 20 Vauxhall Bridge Road, London SW1V 2SA

The authorised representative in the EEA is
Dorling Kindersley Verlag GmbH. Arnulfstr.
124, 80636 Munich, Germany

DK Publishing, 1745 Broadway,
20th Floor, New York, NY 10019, USA

25 26 27 28 10 9 8 7 6 5 4 3 2 1

A CIP catalogue record is available from the British Library.

A catalogue record for this book is available from the Library of Congress.

ISBN 978 0 2417 8465 5

Printed and bound in China

www.dk.com

MIX
Paper | Supporting responsible forestry
FSC™ C018179

This book was made with Forest Stewardship Council™ certified paper – one small step in DK's commitment to a sustainable future.

Learn more at **www.dk.com/uk/information/sustainability**

WELCOME TO BERLIN

There's truly nowhere else like Berlin. Home to a vibrant cultural scene, distinct and diverse neighbourhoods and an intriguing but chequered history, there's enough here to fill the busiest of itineraries. Whatever your dream trip to Berlin includes, this DK Mini Map and Guide is the perfect travel companion.

The former capital of Prussia and a European stronghold, Berlin has long been a city of great significance. Its fascinating and difficult past is still very much evident today, from the disused Gestapo headquarters at the Topography of Terror to Unter den Linden, dotted with glorious Neo-Classical and Baroque buildings. This leafy boulevard is anchored in the west by the magnificent 18th-century Brandenburg Gate, an iconic symbol of reunification. Berliners celebrated the fall of the Berlin Wall here, and its presence today serves as a reminder that the city was divided into East and West for 28 years.

Perhaps an antidote to the darker chapters of its recent history, hedonism thrives here. Berlin is a natural playground for night owls, and it's almost too easy to get lost in its gritty dive bars and infamous clubs. The city charms early birds, too. Browse local flea markets for vintage treasure and swing by Urban Spree's edgy street-art galleries, or lean into Berlin's quieter, greener side by following walking trails in sprawling Tiergarten or around Potsdam's regal parks. Natural beauty can also be found at sparkling lake Wannsee, the ideal location for a refreshing swim.

In a city with endless opportunities, it can be hard to know where to start. We've broken down Berlin into easily navigable chapters, highlighting each area's unmissable sights and unexpected delights. Add insider tips, a comprehensive fold-out map and a need-to-know section full of expert advice for before and during your trip, and you've got an indispensable guidebook. Enjoy the book, and enjoy Berlin.

↓ The Brandenburg Gate bathed by the setting sun

AROUND UNTER DEN LINDEN

Berlin's most stately street still fulfils its role as a connecting artery between Museumsinsel and Tiergarten park. Lined with some of the city's most impressive Baroque and Neo-Classical buildings, this is the boulevard you'll want to stroll down for a first impression of Berlin: both its Prussian past and its cosmopolitan present.

↓ Schiller's Monument and the Deutscher Dom

The Zeughaus building, and the exhibition hall extension designed by I M Pei *(inset)*

ZEUGHAUS (DHM)

V3 Unter den Linden 2 S & U Friedrichstrasse, Museumsinsel S Hackescher Markt 100, 300 10am-6pm daily dhm.de

This stunning Baroque building houses the Deutsches Historisches Museum (German History Museum), which explores the history of Germany through a fascinating collection of art, militaria and crafts.

Located in Berlin's historic district of Mitte, the Zeughaus was built as the armoury of the Prussian army in the 18th century. It is a magnificent structure; its wings surround an inner courtyard and the exterior is decorated with Schlüter's sculptures depicting mythological giants. Since 1952 it has housed the Deutsches Historisches Museum (DHM), which has a permanent exhibition of over one million objects about German history. The museum was founded in 1987 on the occasion of the 750th anniversary of Berlin. With the reunification of Germany in 1990, the buildings and collections of East Germany (officially the German Democratic Republic) came into the hands of the German History Museum, and the collections representing the history of all the parts of Germany moved into the Zeughaus. In 2003, a strikingly curvaceous, glass-walled exhibition hall was added, designed by Walter Gropius student I M Pei. Its four different levels are used for temporary exhibitions about significant historical events.

GALLERY GUIDE

The ground floor houses exhibits from 1918 to the present. The first floor contains collections dating from early civilizations and the Middle Ages right up to the beginning of the 20th century. A subterranean pathway links the Zeughaus to the temporary shows in the exhibition hall.

EXPERIENCE MORE

Maxim Gorki Theater

V2 Am Festungsgraben 2 20 22 11 15 S & U Friedrichstrasse S Unter den Linden U Museumsinsel 100, 300 M1

The Maxim Gorki theatre was once a singing school or *Sing-Akademie*. Berlin's oldest concert hall, it was built in 1827 by Carl Theodor Ottmer, who based his design on drawings by Karl Friedrich Schinkel. This modest Neo-Classical building, with its attractive façade resembling a Greco-Roman temple, was well known for the excellent acoustic qualities of its concert hall.

Many famous composer-musicians have performed here, including the violinist Niccolò Paganini and pianist Franz Liszt. In 1829, Felix Mendelssohn-Bartholdy conducted a performance of the *St Matthew Passion* by Johann Sebastian Bach here. It was the first time that the work had been performed in front of an audience since the composer's death in 1750. Following reconstruction after World War II, the building became a theatre.

Neue Wache

V3 Unter den Linden 4 S Hackescher Markt U Museumsinsel 100, 300 10am-6pm daily

This war memorial, designed by Karl Friedrich Schinkel and built in the 1810s, is one of the finest examples of Neo-Classical architecture in Berlin. Its façade is dominated by a huge Doric portico with a frieze of bas-reliefs depicting goddesses of victory. On the triangular tympanum above the pediment are allegorical representations of Battle, Victory, Flight and Defeat.

In the 1930s the building, originally a royal guard-house, was turned into a monument to soldiers killed during World War I. In 1960, following its restoration, Neue Wache became the Memorial to the Victims of Fascism and Militarism. In 1993 it was again rededicated, this time to the memory of all victims of war and dictatorship.

Inside the building is a granite slab over the ashes of an unknown soldier, a resistance fighter and a concentration camp prisoner. Under the circular opening in the roof is a copy of the 20th-century sculpture *Mother with her Dead Son*, by Berlin artist Käthe Kollwitz, who lost her own son in World War I.

Neo-Classical façade of the Neue Wache

Staatsbibliothek

U3 Unter den Linden 8 S & U Friedrichstrasse U Unter den Linden 100, 300 9am-9pm Mon-Fri, 10am-5pm Sat staatsbibliothek-berlin.de

The nucleus of the State Library collection was the library of the Great Elector, Friedrich Wilhelm, founded in 1661, first situated in the Stadtschloss and later moved to the Alte Bibliothek building. Its current home was designed by Ernst von Ihne and completed in 1914 on the site of the Academy of Science and the Academy of Fine Arts. This impressive building was severely damaged during World War II and underwent extensive restoration. The collection, of some three million books and periodicals, was scattered during the war. A collection of priceless music manuscripts ended up in the Jagiellonian Library in Krakow, Poland.

After the war, only part of the collection was returned to the building in Unter den Linden, and the rest was held in West Berlin. Since reunification, both collections are once again under the same administration.

Altes Palais

V3 Unter den Linden 9 U Museumsinsel, Unter den Linden 100, 300

The Neo-Classical Old Palace, near the former Opernplatz (Bebelplatz), was built for the heir to the throne – Prince Wilhelm (later Kaiser Wilhelm I). The Kaiser lived here all his life. He was able to watch the changing of the guards every day from the ground-floor window on the far left.

The palace, built in the 1830s, was designed by the architect Carl Ferdinand Langhans. Its splendid furnishings were destroyed during World War II but the palace was subsequently restored and is now used by Humboldt Universität.

Palais am Festungsgraben

V2 Am Festungsgraben 1 618 14 60 S Friedrichstrasse U Museumsinsel 100, 300 M1

The Festungsgraben Palace is one of the few structures in this part of town that retains its original interior décor. Built as a small Baroque palace in 1753, it owes its present form to major extension work, carried out in 1864 in the style of Karl Friedrich Schinkel, by Heinrich Bürde and Hermann von der Hude.

The late Neo-Classical style of the building is reminiscent of Schinkel's later designs. The interior includes a magnificent double-height marble hall in the Neo-Renaissance style, which was modelled on the White Room in the former Stadtschloss. In 1934 one room was turned into a music salon, and musical instruments were brought here from the 19th-century house (now demolished) of manufacturer Johann Weydinger (1773–1837). The palace is now used for private events.

EAT

Augustiner am Gendarmenmarkt

Hearty German fare (knuckle of pork, beef goulash) can be found at this Bavarian pub, which overlooks the Gendarmenmarkt, one of Berlin's most beautiful squares.

U4 Charlottenstrasse 55 204 540 20

Reiterdenkmal Friedrichs des Grossen

V3 Unter den Linden Museumsinsel, Unter den Linden 100, 300

This equestrian statue of Frederick the Great is one of the most famous monuments in Berlin, featuring the massive 5.6-m- (18.5-ft-) high bronze statue standing on the centre lane of Unter den Linden. It was designed by Christian Daniel Rauch and completed in 1851. It depicts Frederick the Great on horseback, wearing a uniform and a royal cloak. The base of the high plinth is surrounded by statues of famous military leaders, politicians, scientists and artists.

The top tier of the plinth is decorated with bas-relief scenes from the life of Frederick the Great. Out of line with GDR ideology, the monument was moved to Potsdam, where it stood by the Hippodrome in Park Sanssouci until its return in 1980.

Pierre Boulez Saal

V3 Französische Strasse 33D Unter den Linden, Hausvogteiplatz 100, 147 M1, M12 Hours vary, check website boulezsaal.de

This concert hall opened in 2017 as part of the Barenboim-Said Akademie – an institution formed in continuation of Edward Said and Daniel Barenboim's West-Eastern Divan Orchestra to focus on music education in the humanistic tradition of the orchestra. American architect Frank Gehry has given the Pierre Boulez Saal impeccable acoustics and an intimate layout that ensures that no audience member is more than 14 m (50 ft) from the conductor. The hall hosts a diverse chamber music programme throughout the year, featuring both orchestras and soloists, with regular performances from the in-house Boulez Ensemble. There are also concerts for children.

Staatsoper Unter den Linden

V3 Unter den Linden 7 Museumsinsel, Unter den Linden 100, 300 Hours vary, check website staatsoper-berlin.de

The early Neo-Classical façade of the State Opera House is one of the most beautiful sights along Unter den Linden. It was built by Georg Wenzeslaus von Knobelsdorff in 1741–3, but has been rebuilt and restored several times: in the 1840s after a fire, after World War II and after water damage in the GDR era. The latest works, completed in 2017, resulted in magical acoustics and much more comfortable seats. The building is the home of the Berlin State Opera and

Frederick the Great astride his bronze steed

€400 m

The refurbishment cost of the Staatsoper: almost double the original estimate.

has hosted stellar singers, musicians and artists; one of its directors was Richard Strauss. Audiences can expect Baroque opera as well as new productions.

Humboldt Universität

V3 Unter den Linden 6 20930 S & U Friedrichstrasse U Museumsinsel, Unter den Linden 100, 300

The university building was constructed in 1753 for Prince Heinrich of Prussia, the brother of Frederick the Great. The university was founded in 1810 on the initiative of Wilhelm von Humboldt. It became the Berlin University but was renamed in von Humboldt's honour in 1949.

The overall design of the palace, with its main block and the courtyard enclosed within a pair of wings, has been extended many times. Two marble statues (1883) by Paul Otto stand at the entrance gate and represent Wilhelm von Humboldt (holding a book) and his brother Alexander, a well-known naturalist and traveller (sitting on a globe). The entrance gate leads to the courtyard, designed by Reinhold Begas.

Many renowned scholars have worked at the university, including philosophers Fichte and Hegel, physicians Rudolf Virchow and Robert Koch, and physicists Max Planck and Albert Einstein. Among its graduates are Heinrich Heine, Karl Marx and Friedrich Engels.

After World War II, the university was in the Russian sector of the divided city and the difficulties encountered by the students of the western zone led to the establishment of a new university in 1948 – the Freie Universität.

Kronprinzenpalais

V3 Unter den Linden 3 U Museumsinsel 100, 300

The striking, late Neo-Classical Crown Prince's Palace takes its name from its original inhabitants – the heirs to the royal, and later to the imperial, throne. Its form is the outcome of numerous changes made to what was originally a modest house dating from 1669. The first extensions, designed in the late Baroque style, were conducted by Philipp Gerlach in the 1730s. Between 1856 and 1857 Johann Heinrich Strack added the second floor. These extensions were rebuilt following World War II.

The palace served the royal family until the abolition of the monarchy. Under Communist rule, it was renamed Palais Unter den Linden and reserved for official government guests. It was here, on 31 August 1990, that the pact was signed paving the way for reunification to begin.

Next to the palace, at Unter den Linden 1, is where the Kommandantur, the official quarters of the city's garrison commander, once stood. Totally destroyed during the last days of World War II, the original façade was rebuilt in 2003 by the giant German media company Bertelsmann, as part of their Berlin headquarters. Today, the building is mainly used for staging large exhibitions. Joined to the main palace by an overhanging passageway is the smaller Prinzessinnenpalais (Princesses' Palace), built for the daughters of Friedrich Wilhelm III. Today, behind the Baroque façade, a modern venue called PalaisPopulaire displays the Deutsche Bank's art collection. The ground-floor café, LePopulaire, offers traditional coffee and cake with stunning view of Berlin's landmarks.

St-Hedwigs-Kathedrale

V3 Bebelplatz S & U Hausvogteiplatz, Museumsinsel, Unter den Linden 100, 300 Hours vary, check website W hedwigs-kathedrale.de

The massive church of St Hedwig, set back from the road and crowned with a copper dome, is the Catholic Cathedral of the Roman Archdiocese of Berlin. It was built to serve the Catholics of Silesia (part of present-day Poland), which became part of the Kingdom of Prussia in 1742 following defeat in the Silesian Wars of 1740–63.

The initial design, by Georg Wenzeslaus von Knobelsdorff, was similar to the Roman Pantheon. Construction began in 1747 and the cathedral was consecrated in 1773, although work continued on and off until 1778. Later, additional work was carried out from 1886 to 1887. The cathedral was badly damaged during World War II, and rebuilt between 1952 and 1963. Major renovations between 2019 and 2024 saw the altar move directly under the dome. The crypt holds the tombs of many bishops of Berlin. It is also the resting place of Bernhard Lichtenberg (1875–1943), a priest killed in a concentration camp and beatified as a martyr by Pope John Paul II.

Did You Know?

Many of the trees on Unter den Linden were chopped down for firewood during World War II.

Unter den Linden

U3 S & U Brandenburger Tor U Unter den Linden 100, 300

One of the most famous streets in Berlin, Unter den Linden starts at Schlossplatz and runs down to the Brandenburg Gate and Pariser Platz. It was once the route to the royal hunting grounds that were later transformed into the Tiergarten. In the 17th century the street was planted with lime trees, to which it owes its name. The current trees were planted in the 1950s.

During the 18th century, Unter den Linden became the main street of the westward-growing city. It was gradually filled with prestigious buildings, many of which were restored after World War II. Today it also has several cafés and restaurants, as well as many smart shops. This street is also the venue for many interesting outdoor events; it is usually crowded with tourists and students browsing the bookstalls around the Humboldt Universität and the Staatsbibliothek.

Komische Oper

U3 Behrenstrasse 55/57 S & U Brandenburger Tor U Unter den Linden 100, 147, 300 W komische-oper-berlin.de

Looking at the modern façade of the Comic Opera theatre, it is hard to believe that it hides one of Berlin's most impressive interiors. Built in 1892, it has served as

←

Lime (linden) trees on Unter den Linden

a variety theatre and as the German National Theatre, and has only housed the Komische Oper since World War II. The postwar reconstruction deprived the building of its former façades but the beautiful Viennese Neo-Baroque interior remained, full of stuccoes and gilded ornaments. Particularly interesting are the statues on the pilasters of the top balcony by Theodor Friedel. The Komische Oper is one of Berlin's three leading opera companies, presenting contemporary renditions of musicals, operas and operettas. Extensive renovation has been ongoing since 2023 so performances are temporarily being held at different venues across the city. For more information, check the website.

Alte Bibliothek

V3 Bebelplatz 1 20 930 Unter den Linden 100, 300

The Old Library, known by locals as the *Kommode* or "chest of drawers" after its curved façade, is one of the city's most beautiful Baroque buildings. It was designed by Georg Christian Unger and built around 1775 to house the royal library collection. Unger based his design on an unrealized plan for an extension to the Hofburg complex in Vienna by Josef Emanuel Fischer von Erlach some 50 years earlier. The concave façade of the building is accentuated by the insertion of three breaks, surrounded at the top by a row of massive Corinthian pilasters. The building now houses the law faculty of Humboldt University.

Französischer Dom

V4 Gendarmenmarkt 6 Stadtmitte, Hausvogteiplatz Hours vary, check website franzoesischer-dom.de

The French Cathedral stands facing its German counterpart, the Deutscher Dom, across the Gendarmenmarkt square. It was built for the French Huguenot community, who found refuge in Protestant Berlin following their expulsion from France after the revocation of the Edict of Nantes. The main building of the church, completed in 1705, was modelled on the Huguenot church in Charenton, France, which was destroyed in 1688.

The structure is dominated by a massive, cylindrical tower, which is encircled by Corinthian porticoes at its base. It was added around 1785, some 80 years after the church was built. In 1987, a viewing platform and large carillon were incorporated to celebrate Berlin's 750th anniversary. It also houses the Huguenot Museum, which details the history of the Huguenots in France and Brandenburg. Well-educated and highly skilled, they played a crucial part in Berlin's rise as a city of science, craft and commerce. The French language they brought with them survives to this day in many words used in the Berlin dialect.

→

Main entrance of the Französischer Dom, built for the dispossessed French Huguenots

Konzerthaus

V4 Gendarmenmarkt 2 Stadtmitte, Hausvogteiplatz konzerthaus.de

A late Neo-Classical jewel, the magnificent Concert Hall, formerly known as the Schauspielhaus, is one of the greatest achievements of Berlin's best-known architect, Karl Friedrich Schinkel.

It was built between 1818 and 1821 around the ruins of Carl Gotthard Langhans' National Theatre, which was destroyed by fire in 1817. The original portico columns were retained. Schinkel was responsible for the architectural structure and for the interior design, down to the door handles. Following bomb damage in World War II, it was reconstructed as a concert hall with a different interior layout. The exterior was restored to its former glory. The Konzerthaus is home to the Konzerthausorchester (formerly the Berlin Symphony Orchestra).

The theatre façade includes a huge Ionic portico with a set of stairs that was only used by the middle classes (the upper classes entered via a separate entrance where they could leave their horse-drawn carriages). The whole building is richly decorated with sculptures alluding to drama and music: statues of musical geniuses mounted on lions and panthers, as well as figures representing the Muses and a Bacchanal procession. The façade is crowned with the sculpture of Apollo riding a chariot pulled by griffins.

In front of the theatre stands a shining white marble statue of the poet and philosopher Friedrich Schiller. It was sculpted by Reinhold Begas, and erected in 1869. Removed by the Nazis during the 1930s, the monument was finally returned to its rightful place in 1988.

Deutscher Dom

V4 Gendarmenmarkt 1 Stadtmitte, Hausvogteiplatz 22 73 04 31 May-Sep: 10am-7pm Tue-Sun; Oct-Apr: 10am-6pm Tue-Sun

The German Cathedral at the southern end of Gendarmenmarkt, to the left of the Konzerthaus, is an old German Protestant-Reformed church built in 1708 by Giovanni Simonetti. The design was based on a five-petal shape, and in 1785 it acquired a dome-covered tower identical to that of the French Cathedral across the square. Burned down in 1945, the church was rebuilt in 1993. Its exterior was painstakingly reconstructed, including its sculpted decorations. The interior is now modern and hosts an exhibition, *"Wege, Irrwege, Umwege"* ("Paths, Confusions, Detours"), about Germany's parliamentary democracy.

SHOP

Annette Görtz

This boutique store by German designer Annette Görtz sells timeless fashion pieces, fine knitwear and modern accessories for women.

V3 Markgrafenstrasse 42 11am-7pm Mon-Fri, 10am-7pm Sat annettegoertz.net

The Square Berlin East

This upscale design store sells exclusive lifestyle and fashion products.

V3 Französische Strasse 40 10:30am-7pm Mon-Sat thesquareberlin.de

Friedrichstadt-passagen

U4 Friedrichstrasse Quartier 205, 206, 207 Stadtmitte, Hausvogteiplatz

This group of passages is part of a massive development of shops, offices, restaurants and apartments built along Friedrichstrasse.

Quartier 207 is the former home of Galeries Lafayette, a branch of the French department store. Although this charming building, constructed almost entirely of glass, was designed by Jean Nouvel to house a shopping complex, it is awaiting a new purpose now. The building's axis is formed by an inner courtyard, which is defined by two glass cones with their bases facing each other. The highly reflective glass panes, together with the multi-coloured stands that are clustered around the structure, make an extraordinary impression on the visitor.

The next passage, Quartier 206, has offices, a private medical centre as well as some stores. It is the work of the American design team Pei Cobb Freed & Partners. The building owes its alluring, but somewhat nouveau-riche, appearance to the use of forms inspired by Art Deco architecture, including sophisticated details and expensive stone cladding.

The southernmost building in the complex, and the largest passage, is Quartier 205 – now called "The Q" – another complex of shops, designed by Oswald Mathias Ungers.

Cold War Black Box

U5 Friedrichstrasse 47 Stadtmitte, Kochstrasse M29 10am-6pm daily bfgg.de

Located directly across from the Haus am Checkpoint Charlie, the Cold War Black Box provides a quieter, more measured look at the Cold War years. Throughout its intimate, black-walled space, it tackles big-hitter topics such as nuclear war and espionage, as well as peace and democracy.

The exhibition comprises around 500 items, including GDR-era grenades once used for practice by school children, a machine to measure radioactivity and a Soviet photo gun used for reconnaissance missions. There are also many media stations with film excerpts, interviews, photos, and explorations of international connections with the Korean War and the Cuban missile crisis.

Gendarmenmarkt

V4 Stadtmitte, Hausvogteiplatz

This is one of Berlin's most beautiful squares, created at the end of the 17th century as a marketplace for the newly established Friedrichstadt. It is named after the Regiment Gens d'Armes, who stabled their horses here. Two cathedrals with magnificient towers, the Deutscher Dom and the Französischer Dom, stand on each side with the Konzerthaus in the middle.

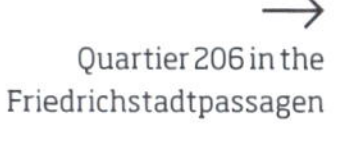

→ Quartier 206 in the Friedrichstadtpassagen

Holocaust Denkmal

S/T4 Ebertstrasse 28 04 59 60 & Brandenburger Tor 100, 300 Apr-Sep: 10am-8pm Tue-Sun; Oct-Mar: 10am-7pm Tue-Sun Mon

The Holocaust memorial for the six million Jewish people and others murdered by the Nazis in concentration camps between 1933 and 1945 was inaugurated in 2005. It is a 19,000-sq-m (205,000-sq-ft) site containing 2,711 concrete slabs or "stelae" of varying heights, arranged in an austere grid pattern on a sloping field. The abstract installation is intended to disorientate, and leaves room for interpretation. There is also an information centre beneath the memorial that displays the names of around three million Jewish Holocaust victims.

Bahnhof Friedrichstrasse

U2 Reichstagufer 17 9am-7pm Tue-Fri, 10am-6pm Sat & Sun hdg.de

One of the city's most famous urban railway stations, Bahnhof Friedrichstrasse used to be the border station between East and West Berlin during the Cold War years.

It was built in 1882 to a design by Johannes Vollmer. In 1925 a roof was added, covering the hall and the platforms. The original labyrinth of passages, staircases and checkpoints no longer exists but it is possible to see a model of the station at the Stasi-Museum.

The only remaining structure from the original station is the special pavilion once used as a waiting room by those waiting for emigration clearance. It earned the nickname Tränenpalast, the "Palace of Tears", as it is here that Berliners from different sides of the city would say goodbye to each other after a visit. Today, it is home to a small museum that looks at what the partition of Germany meant for Berliners.

Museum für Kommunikation

U5 Leipziger Strasse 16 Stadtmitte, Anton-Wilhelm-Amo-Strasse 200, 265, M48 9am-8pm Tue, 9am-5pm Wed-Fri, 10am-6pm Sat & Sun mfk-berlin.de

Founded in 1872 as the Post Office Museum, the Museum of Communication is the oldest establishment of its kind in the entire world. Soon after it was founded, it moved into the corner of the huge building constructed for the main post office. The office wings, with their

modest Neo-Renaissance elevations, contrast with the grand Neo-Baroque façade. Exhibits illustrate the history of postal and telecommunication services, including contemporary digital media.

Akademie der Künste

T3 Pariser Platz 4 S & U Brandenburger Tor 100, 300 10am-10pm daily adk.de

The modern glass and steel façade of the Academy of Arts belies its historic and noble origins. Founded in 1696 by Prussian King Frederick I, it was one of Europe's first such institutions. Today its primary role is advising and supporting the German government in affairs of art and culture. It also houses a prestigious archive and hosts contemporary art exhibitions.

←
A small corner of the massive Holocaust Denkmal

Ehemaliges Regierungsviertel

T5 Wilhelmstrasse, Leipziger Strasse, Voss Strasse U Potsdamer Platz, Anton-Wilhelm-Amo-Strasse

The name means "former government district", because Wilhelmstrasse, and the area to the west of it up to Leipziger Platz, was where the main government departments had offices from the mid-19th century until 1945. The building at Voss Strasse No. 77 was once the Reich's Chancellery and Otto von Bismarck's office, and from 1933 it served as the office of Adolf Hitler. From here Hitler, his senior staff and his mistress Eva Braun withdrew to the Führerbunker, an underground complex that served as command centre and residence. In the spring of 1945 the square was the scene of such fierce fighting that after World War II most of the damaged buildings had to be torn down. Among those that survived are the former Prussian Landtag offices – the huge complex occupying the site between Leipziger and Niederkirchner Strasse. This building, designed in the Italian Renaissance style, was designed by Friedrich Schulze, and constructed between 1892 and 1904. It consists of two segments: the section on the side of Leipziger Strasse (No. 3–4) once had the upper chamber of the National Assembly (the Herrenhaus) and is now used by the Bundesrat. The building on the side of Niederkirchner Strasse (No. 5) is the former seat of the Landtag's lower chamber, and is now the Berliner Abgeordnetenhaus (House of Representatives).

The other surviving complex is the former Ministry of Aviation, at Leipziger Strasse No. 5, built for Hermann Göring in 1936 by Ernst Sagebiel. This building is typical of the architecture of the Third Reich.

FÜHRERBUNKER

The specific location of Hitler's bunker was kept a secret for decades to deter neo-Nazi pilgrims. Destroyed and flooded after World War II, the area now hosts a car parking area and some GDR-era residential buildings. An information board installed by the nonprofit Berliner Unterwelten group (which runs tours of other bunkers and subterranean historic sites throughout the city) shows the layout of the structure.

Russische Botschaft

T3 Unter den Linden 63/65 S&U Brandenburger Tor 100, 200

The monumental white Russian Embassy building is an example of the Stalinist "wedding-cake" style, or *Zuckerbäckerstil*. Completed in 1953, it was the first postwar building erected on Unter den Linden. It is built on the site of a former palace that had housed the Russian (originally Tsarist) embassy from 1837.

The work of Russian architect Anatoli Strischewski, this imposing structure, with its strictly symmetrical layout, resembles the old Berlin palaces of the Neo-Classical period. The sculptures that adorn it, however, belong to an altogether different era: the gods of ancient Greece and Rome have been replaced by working-class heroes.

Asisi Panorama Berlin

U5 Friedrichstrasse 205 S&U Potsdamer Platz U Stadtmitte, Kochstrasse M48, M29 10am-6pm daily asisi.de

Turkish-German artist Yadegar Asisi paints enormous, highly detailed panoramas known for their sense of realism. His Berlin panorama is 15 m (49 ft) high, 60 m (196 ft) wide and set inside a large cylindrical structure next to Checkpoint Charlie. It depicts a fictional day along a stretch of the Berlin Wall in the 1980s. On one side is Kreuzberg, complete with punks, run-down buildings and daily West Berlin life; on the other side, an eerily quiet Mitte, all border fortifications, no people and the TV tower looming in the distance. With a soundtrack by film composer Eric Babak, the experience is absorbing and unexpectedly moving.

Brandenburger Tor

S3 Pariser Platz S&U Brandenburger Tor 100, 245

The Brandenburg Gate is the quintessential symbol of Berlin. This magnificent Neo-Classical structure, completed in 1795, was designed by Carl Gotthard Langhans and modelled on the entrance to the Acropolis in Athens. A pair of pavilions, once used by guards and customs officers, frames its powerful Doric colonnade. The bas-reliefs depict scenes from Greek mythology, and the whole structure is crowned by the Quadriga sculpture designed by Johann Gottfried Schadow. The goddess of victory with her four-horsed chariot

Brandenburger Tor dominating Pariser Platz ↑

was originally regarded as a symbol of peace. In 1806, during the French occupation, the Quadriga was dismantled on Napoleon's orders and taken to Paris. On its return in 1814, it was declared a symbol of victory, and the goddess received the staff bearing the Prussian eagle and the iron cross adorned with a laurel wreath. The Brandenburg Gate has borne witness to many of Berlin's important events, from military parades to celebrations marking the birth of the Third Reich and Hitler's ascent to power. It was here, too, that the Russian flag was raised in May 1945, and on 17 June 1953 that 25 workers demonstrating for better conditions were killed. The gate, in East Berlin, was

restored during 1956–8, after it suffered extensive damage in World War II. Until 1989 it stood watch over the divided city. It was restored again between 2000 and 2002.

Pariser Platz

T3 S & U Brandenburger Tor 100, 245

This square, at the end of Unter den Linden, was created in 1734. Originally called Quarré, it was renamed Pariser Platz after 1814, when the Quadriga sculpture from the Brandenburg Gate was returned to Berlin from Paris. The square, bordered on the west by the Brandenburg Gate, saw most of its buildings destroyed in 1945. Following reunification, the square was redeveloped, and twin houses designed by Josef Paul Kleihues now flank the Brandenburg Gate. On the north side of the square are the Dresdner Bank building and the French Embassy. On the south are the US Embassy, the DZ Bank head office and the Academy of Fine Arts. To the east is the rebuilt Hotel Adlon, a legend in Berlin hospitality.

Admiralspalast

U2 Friedrichstrasse 101-102 25 50 70 00 S & U Friedrichstrasse

The Admiralspalast, built in 1911, was one of the Roaring Twenties' premier entertainment complexes in Berlin, and one of the many variety and vaudeville theatres that once lined Friedrichstrasse. Originally designed as an indoor swimming pool above a natural hot spring, it was later transformed into an ice-skating rink and, after heavy damage in World War II, an *Operettentheater* that staged light musical entertainment.

In 2006, following restoration work, the theatre reopened with a production of Bertolt Brecht's *Die Dreigroschenoper* (*The Threepenny Opera*), and is once again a vibrant entertainment complex, with a large stage, a café and a nightclub. Designed by Heinrich Schweitzer, the beautifully restored façade is punctuated by Doric half-columns and inlaid with slabs of Istrian marble. The façade on Planckstrasse, designed by Ernst Westphal, features exotic overlapping motifs.

MUSEUMSINSEL

At the heart of Berlin's central Mitte district is a long island nestled in the tributaries of the winding river Spree. The UNESCO-listed museum complex on this island is one of Berlin's unique landmarks and a must-see for anyone interested in art and history. And when you're done exploring the museums, the rest of the city is only a short walk away.

Fountain at the entrance of the Alte Nationalgalerie

↑ The museum building, designed by Friedrich August Stüler

Sarcophagi from the Egyptian Museum and Papyrus Collection →

NEUES MUSEUM

V2 Bodestrasse 1-3 Hackescher Markt, Friedrichstrasse Museumsinsel 100, 300 12, M1, M4, M5 Jul & Aug: 9am-8pm Tue-Sun, 9am-6pm Sun; Sep-Jun: 10am-6pm Tue-Sun; book in advance via website smb.museum

The museum is home to an unparalleled collection of Berlin's archaeological treasures from around the world. Through its exhibits, visitors can explore human history and culture from prehistoric times to the Middle Ages.

The New Museum was built in the mid-19th century to relieve the overcrowded Altes Museum. In 1945, the building was badly damaged, but the reconstruction effort under British architect David Chipperfield – a skilful blend of conservation, restoration and creation of new spaces – was highly successful, and history remains palpable in every room.

The two main collections are the Egyptian Museum and Papyrus Collection and the Museum for Prehistory and Early History. The former showcases four millennia of ancient Egyptian and Nubian cultures, while the latter focuses on Europe and parts of Asia. Special themes and items include 19th-century wall paintings of Nordic mythological scenes, Heinrich Schliemann's collection of artifacts from Troy, the Neanderthal from Le Moustier, the Berlin Gold Hat and a bust of Nefertiti.

BERLINER DOM

W2 Am Lustgarten Hackescher Markt 100, 300 9am-8pm daily (winter: to 7pm), noon-8pm Sun & public hols berlinerdom.de

Standing on the east bank of the Spree, Berlin Cathedral is singled out from its neighbours on Museumsinsel, allowing visitors to fully take in this awe-inspiring city landmark.

The original Berliner Dom was completed in 1750, based on a modest Baroque design by Johann Boumann. The present Neo-Baroque structure is the work of Julius Raschdorff and dates from 1894–1905. The central copper dome is some 98 m (321 ft) high. Following severe World War II damage, the cathedral has been restored in a simplified form but still contains some original features like the pulpit and altar.

Sauer's Organ contains some 7,200 pipes.

270

The number of steps up to the dome's walkway, with great views over Museumsinsel.

Hidden beneath the floor, the Imperial Hohenzollern family crypt contains 100 richly decorated sarcophagi.

Must See

GREAT VIEW
Light Show

For ten days in October, Berlin gets a kaleidoscopic remix during the annual Festival of Lights, when famous sights like the Berliner Dom become canvases for creative light shows.

↑ Façade of the cathedral transformed by changing light and video projections during the Festival of Lights

The mosaics inside the dome contain over half a million tiles each.

↑ The Berliner Dom, a Neo-Baroque cathedral dating back to 1750

↑ The impressive Neo-Renaissance interior featuring some extravagant furnishings and impressive decorations

DOME MOSAICS

Look up at the interior of the dome to marvel at Anton von Werner's intricate mosaics. All but destroyed during World War II, von Werner's original designs were used by Tuscan company Ferrari & Bacci to reproduce the mosaics between 1975 and 2002.

PERGAMONMUSEUM

V2 Am Kupfergraben 5 Hackescher Markt, Friedrichstrasse Museumsinsel 100, 300 12, M1 For renovation until spring 2027 smb.museum

This unique museum is home to a magnificent collection of large architectural treasures excavated by German archaeologists in the late 19th century. The exhibits are as awe-inspiring for their fabulous designs as for their grand scale.

Built between 1910 and 1930 to a design by Alfred Messel and Ludwig Hoffmann, this museum houses one of Europe's most famous collections of antiquities. The three independent collections – the Collection of Classical Antiquities (Greek and Roman), the Museum of the Ancient Near East and the Museum of Islamic Art – are the result of intensive archaeological excavations by late 19th- and early 20th-century German expeditions to the Near and Middle East. Due to renovation work, this museum is completely closed to the public. The north wing, which contains the Pergamon Altar, is scheduled to reopen in 2027. Construction in the south wing will continue until 2037.

The Pergamonmuseum backs on to the river Spree

JAMES-SIMON-GALERIE

The museum, once it reopens, can only be entered via the James-Simon-Galerie. This new entrance building, designed by David Chipperfield and named after patron James Simon (1851–1932), serves as a central reception area for the visitors of Museumsinsel. It also has an area for temporary exhibitions and a museum shop.

↑ The reconstructed Pergamon Altar, and *(inset)* a detail of one of its friezes from the Antikensammlung collection

The wedge-shaped Bode-Museum on Museumsinsel

EXPERIENCE MORE

Bode-Museum

V2 Monbijoubrücke (Bodestrasse 1-3) Hackescher Markt, Friedrichstrasse 100, 147, 300 12, M1, M4, M5, M6 10am-5pm Wed-Fri, 10am-6pm Sat & Sun smb.museum

The Bode-Museum building was designed in the 1890s by Ernst von Ihne to fit the wedge-shaped end of the island. The interior was designed with the help of an art historian, Wilhelm von Bode, who was the director of the Berlin state museums at the time. The museum, which opened in 1904, displayed a rather mixed collection that included some Old Masters. Its original name, Kaiser Friedrich Museum, was changed after World War II. Following the reassembling of the Berlin collections, all of the paintings were put in the Gemäldegalerie. The Egyptian art and the papyrus collection were moved to the Ägyptisches Museum (Egyptian Museum) at Charlottenburg. They are now housed at the Neues Museum.

Today, the museum is home to Skulpturensammlung, one of the largest collections of ancient sculptures in the world. Other displays include an outstanding collection of some of the world's oldest coins, including a few from Athens in the 6th century BCE, as well as Roman, medieval and 20th-century coins. There are also sculptures by Tilman Riemenschneider, Donatello, Bernini and Canova.

Alte Nationalgalerie

W2 Bodestrasse 1-3 Hackescher Markt, Friedrichstrasse Museumsinsel 100, 300 12, M1, M4, M5 Hours vary, check website; book in advance online smb.museum

The Old National Gallery was completed in 1876 to a design by Friedrich August Stüler, who took into account the sketches made by Friedrich Wilhelm IV. The building is situated on a high platform reached via a double staircase. On the top stands an equestrian statue of Friedrich Wilhelm IV, the work of Alexander Calandrelli in 1886. Details on the façade reflect the building's purpose – the tympanum features Germania as patron of art, while the top is crowned with a personification of the arts. Originally meant to house modern art, the current gallery includes works of masters such as Adolph von Menzel, Wilhelm Leibl, Max Liebermann and Arnold Böcklin.

There is no shortage of sculptures either, with works by Christian Daniel Rauch, Johann Gottfried Schadow, Antonio Canova and Reinhold Begas. Another two halls display paintings from the German Romantic era, featuring Caspar David Friedrich, Karl Friedrich Schinkel and Karl Blechen.

Altes Museum

W2 Am Lustgarten (Bodestrasse 1-3) Hackescher Markt Museumsinsel 100, 300 10am-5pm Wed-Fri, 10am-6pm Sat & Sun smb.museum

The Old Museum building, designed by Karl Friedrich Schinkel, is a beautiful Neo-Classical structures, with a 87-m- (285-ft-) high portico supported by 18 Ionic columns. Built in 1830 for the royal collection of art and antiquities, it now houses part of Berlin's Collection of Classical Antiquities, with permanent exhibitions on the art and culture of ancient Greece and on Roman and Etruscan art and sculptures.

Lustgarten

W2 Hackescher Markt 100, 300

The enchanting garden in front of the Altes Museum looks as though it has always been there, but in its present form it was established in the late 1990s.

Used to grow vegetables and herbs for the Stadtschloss until the late 16th century, it became a real *Lustgarten* (pleasure garden) in the reign of the Great Elector. However, its statues, grottoes, fountains and vegetation were removed when Friedrich Wilhelm I (1688–1740), known for his love of military pursuits, turned the garden into an army drill ground.

Following the construction of the Altes Museum, the ground became a park, designed by Peter Joseph Lenné. In 1831, it was adorned with a monolithic granite bowl by Christian Gottlieb Cantian, to a design by Schinkel. The 63-tonne (70-ton) bowl, measuring nearly 7 m (23 ft) in diameter, was intended for the museum rotunda, but was too heavy to carry inside. After 1933, the Lustgarten was paved over and turned into a parade ground, remaining as such until 1989. Its current restoration is based on Lenné's original designs.

Did You Know?

Museumsinsel was designated a UNESCO World Heritage Site in 1999.

Schlossbrücke

W3 Hackescher Markt Museumsinsel 100, 300

This is one of the city's most beautiful bridges, connecting Schlossplatz with Unter den Linden. It was built in 1824 to a design by Karl Friedrich Schinkel, who was one of Germany's most influential architects. Statues were added to the top of the bridge's sparkling granite pillars in 1853. These figures were also created by Schinkel and made of stunning white Carrara marble. The statues depict tableaux taken from Greek mythology, for instance Iris, Nike and Athena training and looking after their favourite young warriors.

Remember to take a close look at the wrought-iron balustrade, which is delightfully decorated with intertwined sea creatures.

Marstall

W3 Schlossplatz/ Breite Strasse 36-37 Museumsinsel 147, 200, 248

The buildings of the former Royal Stables form a huge complex, occupying the area between the Spree and Breite Strasse, south of Schlossplatz. The wing on the side of Breite Strasse is a fragment of the old structure built in 1669. It was designed by Michael Matthias Smids and is the only surviving early Baroque building in Berlin. The wings running along Schlossplatz and the Spree river were built much later, in 1901, but are reminiscent of the Berlin Baroque style – probably because von Ihne modelled them on designs by Jean de Bodt from 1700.

Once the imperial home of more than 300 horses, the building now houses the Hanns Eisler Academy of Music and also hosts a branch of the Berlin City Library.

Nicolaihaus

W4 Brüderstrasse 13 20 45 81 63 Spittelmarkt 147, 265, 248

Built around 1670, the Nicolaihaus is a fine example of Baroque architecture, with its original, magnificent oak staircase still in place. The house owes its fame, however, to its time as the home and bookshop of the publisher, writer and critic Christoph Friedrich Nicolai (1733–1811). One of the outstanding personalities of the Berlin Enlightenment, Nicolai was a supporter of such notable cultural figures as the Jewish philosopher Moses Mendelssohn and the playwright Gotthold Ephraim Lessing. Other regular artistic visitors included Johann Gottfried Schadow, Karl Wilhelm Ramler and Daniel Chodowiecki, all commemorated with a wall plaque. Today, the building houses the offices of the German Association of Protected Buildings, and is open to the public only by appointment.

Humboldt Forum

W3 Schlossplatz Hackescher Markt Museumsinsel 100, 200, 300 Exhibitions: 10:30am-6:30pm Wed-Mon; events: 11am-midnight humboldtforum.org

The Humboldt Forum sits on the site of a gigantic residential complex known as the Stadtschloss (City Palace). Built first as a castle in 1451, it served as the main residence of the Brandenburg Electors. Rebuilt in the style of a

The Humboldt Forum overlooking the Spree

DECOLONIZING BERLIN'S MUSEUMS

Many of the Museumsinsel's institutions, including the Pergamonmuseum, the Ethnological Museum and the Humboldt Forum, showcase artifacts from Germany's colonial past. Following controversy in recent years about how European museums should treat pieces acquired under colonialism, several museums have returned African objects stolen or bought during colonial times. In 2020, the German government agreed to publish an online database of museum objects acquired in a colonial context.

three-storey palace in the 16th century, it became the main seat of the Hohenzollern family for almost 500 years until the end of the monarchy. The palace partly burned down during World War II, and in 1950–51, despite protests, the building was demolished. After a lengthy debate, it was decided to rebuild the palace as a museum complex. Three of the sides of the new building, designed by Franco Stella, take inspiration from the façade of the old palace; the eastern side, however, is to a more modern design. This new museum has been named after Berlin's most prominent intellectual figures: Wilhelm and Alexander von Humboldt. It is home to one of the largest ethnological collections in the world. However, there has been debate over the true ownership of the items it holds, many of which were acquired during Germany's colonial era. The museum is trying a new approach when dealing with these objects, including cooperating with artists and scholars from the artifacts' home countries, such as via the Tanzania–Germany: Shared Object Histories? project. This is an issue that affects many of Germany's museums.

Staatsratsgebäude

W3 Schlossplatz 1 S & U Alexanderplatz 100, 147, 200, M48

The former Staatsratsgebäude, an administrative building that was once the seat of the highest state government council of East Germany, was constructed in 1964. While it was once surrounded by other buildings from the GDR-era, they have since been demolished. The Staatsratsgebäude features the remaining original sculptures, including the magnificent atlantes by the famous Dresden sculptor Balthasar Permoser. Their inclusion, however, was not due to their artistic merit, but rather to their propaganda value: it was from the balcony of the portal that Karl Liebknecht proclaimed the birth of the Socialist Republic. Today, the building is home to the Hertie School, which prepares its students for positions in government and civil society.

Galgenhaus

W4 Brüderstrasse 10 206 13 29 13 U Spittelmarkt 147, 248, 265 10am-6pm Mon-Sat

The Gallows House, so named for a local legend in which an innocent woman was hanged, was originally built as the presbytery of the lost church of St Peter. Redesigned in the Neo-Classical style around 1805, the front portal and one room on the ground floor are all that remain of the original Baroque structure. The new building is, however, a delight: perfectly symmetrical, it resembles nothing so much as a dolls' house made life-size.

Today the building houses the commercial Kewenig Gallery, which acquired it in 2013. Before opening, the gallery undertook a major restoration of the building, which shows off the surviving original interior features.

↑ Boats moored at the Historischer Hafen Berlin

branch of the Stadtmuseum Berlin organization, and those who wish to find out more about the history of the city during the museum's ongoing renovation can visit other affiliated museums and monuments such as the Ephraim-Palais. Surrounding the museum is the Köllnischer Park, which has a kennel built in 1928 to house brown bears kept as city mascots, and an unusual statue of Berlin artist Heinrich Zille.

Märkisches Museum

Y4 Am Köllnischen Park 5 S & U Jannowitzbrücke U Märkisches Museum, Heinrich-Heine Strasse 147, 248, 265 For renovation until 2028 W stadtmuseum.de

This architectural pastiche is a complex of red-brick buildings that most resembles a medieval monastery. It was built between 1901 and 1908 to house a collection relating to the history of Berlin and the March of Brandenburg, from the time of the earliest settlers to the present. Inspired by the Brick Gothic style popular in the Bradenburg region, architect Ludwig Hoffmann included references to Wittstock Castle and to St Catherine's Church in the city of Brandenburg. In the entrance hall you'll find a statue of Roland standing guard, which is a copy of the 15th-century monument in the city of Brandenburg. The main hall features the original Gothic portal from the Berlin residence of the Margraves of Brandenburg, which was demolished in 1931. Also featured is one of the original horse's heads from the Schadow Quadriga, which crowns the Brandenburg Gate.

A further collection in the same building is devoted to the Berlin theatre during the period 1730 to 1933, including many posters, old programmes and stage sets. One of the galleries houses some charming old-time mechanical musical instruments, which are played by musicians once a week, at 5pm on Friday, in a special show. The Märkisches Museum is a

Historischer Hafen Berlin

X4 Märkisches Ufer S Jannowitzbrücke U Märkisches Museum, Heinrich-Heine Strasse 147, 248, 265 1-6pm Sat & Sun W historischer-hafen-berlin.de

Moored on the south shore of the island in an area called Fischerinsel, and opposite the Märkisches Ufer, are several examples of boats, barges and tugboats which operated on the Spree river at the end of the 19th century. These craft constitute an open-air museum, the Historic Port of Berlin, which was once located in the Humboldt Port. One of the boats is now used as a café, while another, the *Renate Angelika*, houses a small exhibition on the history of inland waterway transport on the Spree and Havel.

Ermeler-Haus

X4 Märkisches Ufer 10 Märkisches Museum, Heinrich-Heine Strasse 147, 200, 248, 265

With its harmonious Neo-Classical façade, the Ermeler House stands out as one of the most handsome villas in Berlin. This house was once the town residence of Wilhelm Ferdinand Ermeler, a wealthy merchant and shopkeeper who made his money trading in tobacco. It originally stood on Fischerinsel on the opposite bank of the river, at Breite Strasse No. 11, but in 1968 the house was dismantled and reconstructed on this new site. The house was remodelled in 1825 to Ermeler's specifications, with a decor that includes a frieze alluding to aspects of the tobacco business. Restorers have recreated much of the original façade. The Rococo furniture dates from about 1760 and the notable 18th-century staircase has also been rebuilt.

A modern hotel has been built to the rear of the house facing Wallstrasse, using Ermeler-Haus as its kitchens, while the first-floor rooms are used for special events.

Märkisches Ufer

Y4 Märkisches Museum Jannowitzbrücke 147, 248, 265

Once called Neukölln am Wasser (meaning Neukölln on the water), this street, which runs alongside the Spree river, is one of the few corners of Berlin where it is still possible to see the town as it must have looked in the 18th and 19th centuries. Eight pretty houses have been meticulously conserved here. Two Neo-Baroque houses at Nos. 16 and 18, known as Otto-Nagel-Haus, used to contain a small museum displaying paintings by Otto Nagel, a great favourite with the Communist authorities. The building now houses the photo archives for the state museums of Berlin.

A number of pretty garden cafés and fashionable restaurants make this attractive area very popular with tourists.

Ribbeckhaus

W3 Breite Strasse 35 Spittelmarkt 147, 248, M48

Four identical, picturesque gables crown central Berlin's only surviving Renaissance building, the Ribbeck House. It was built around 1624 for Hans Georg von Ribbeck, a court counsellor, who soon sold it to Anna Sophie of Brunswick. After her death in 1659, the house passed to her nephew, Elector Friedrich Wilhelm. As crown property, it later housed various state administrative offices.

The façade has beautiful wrought-iron grilles on the ground-floor windows and a late Renaissance portal, bearing the date and coat of arms of the von Ribbecks. This was replaced in 1960 with a copy, but apart from that, the house is a remarkable example of architectural survival from the city's history.

CÖLLN

An ancient settlement in the area called Fischerinsel at the southern end of Museumsinsel, the village of Cölln with its medieval church has now been razed almost to the ground. Until 1939, however, this working-class area with its tangle of narrow streets maintained a historical character of its own. This vanished completely in the 1960s, when most of the buildings were replaced with tower blocks. A few historical houses, including the Ermeler-Haus, were reconstructed elsewhere, but the atmosphere of this part of town has changed forever.

AROUND ALEXANDERPLATZ

Berlin's most famous square is synonymous with one of the city's most iconic landmarks: the looming GDR-era Fernsehturm. The whole area is characterized by the somewhat dreary – and heritage-protected – Communist buildings that surround it, but it's still the beating heart of Berlin, a place where locals rush by on their morning commute or meet up with friends over the weekend.

Berlin-Alexanderplatz station and the Fernsehturm

ALEXANDERPLATZ

Y2 S & U Alexanderplatz 100, 200, 245, 248, 300 M5, M6, M8 Fernsehturm: Mar-Oct: 9am-midnight daily; Nov-Feb: 10am-midnight daily tv-turm.de

A veritable treasure-trove of Soviet architecture, Alexanderplatz is a bustling square well worth a visit for its shops and restaurants, and to get a taste of the dynamic side of Berlin the locals see every day.

Alexanderplatz, or "Alex" as it is known locally, has a long and tumultuous history, although it is difficult now to find any visible traces of the not-so-recent past. Once called Ochsenmarkt (oxen market), it was the site of a cattle and wool market. It was later renamed after Tsar Alexander I, who visited Berlin in 1805. Houses and shops sprang up along with a market hall and train station, and by the early 20th century "Alex" had become one of the city's busiest spots. In 1929, attempts were made to develop the square, though only two office buildings were added – the Alexanderhaus and the Berolinahaus. These two, both by Peter Behrens, are still standing today. World War II erased most of the square's older buildings and it is now surrounded by 1960s edifices, including the Park Inn and the Fernsehturm.

↑ The World Clock, an iconic city landmark

Fernsehturm

Nearby on Panoramastrasse 1A is the Fernsehturm, or the Television Tower. Nicknamed Telespargel (TV asparagus) by locals, it is the city's tallest structure, at 368 m (1,207 ft), and indeed one of the tallest in Europe. One of the attractions of the tower is the revolving restaurant: a full rotation takes about half an hour, so it is possible to get a bird's-eye view of the whole city while sipping a cup of coffee. On a clear day, visibility can reach up to 40 km (25 miles).

THE FUTURE OF ALEXANDERPLATZ

The plan to breathe some contemporary life into Alexanderplatz goes back to 1993. A mix of factors has consistently thwarted those plans - as has the city's decision to protect some of the Soviet-style buildings as heritage-status structures. However, the Senate has given preliminary approval for three proposed buildings by prominent architect Hans Kollhoff. The new high-rise buildings will have both apartments as well as several commercial establishments. Whether these plans become reality is yet to be seen, but it's the furthest the ideas have got in a quarter of a century.

MARIENKIRCHE

X2 Karl-Liebknecht-Strasse 8 S&U Alexanderplatz 100, 200, 245, 248, 300 M4, M5, M6 10am-6pm daily marienkirche-berlin.de

The church of St Mary is a tranquil, medieval oasis in the heart of Berlin. The early Gothic hall design and the lavish Baroque touches make this one of the most interesting churches in the city.

Marienkirche was first established as a parish church in the second half of the 13th century and construction was completed early in the 14th century. The main building is a long, red-brick Gothic hall, which still contains many beautiful decorations and features dating from the mid-15th to early 18th century, such as the baptismal font (1437) and the pulpit (1703). During reconstruction works in 1380, the church was altered slightly but its overall shape changed only in the 15th century, when it acquired the front tower. In 1790, the tower was crowned with a dome designed by Carl Gotthard Langhans. The church was once hemmed in by buildings, but today it stands alone in the shadow of the Fernsehturm.

The red main hall was built in the Brick Gothic style some time in the mid- to late 13th century

The dome that crowns the tower includes both Baroque and Neo-Gothic elements.

The central part of the Gothic altar, known as the retable, dating from 1510, features three unknown monks.

Totentanz, meaning "dance of death", is the name of a 22-m- (72-ft-) long Gothic wall fresco, dating from 1485.

The Baroque altar, designed by Andreas Krüger around 1762, and *(inset)* sculpture detail from Andreas Schlüter's pulpit, completed in 1703

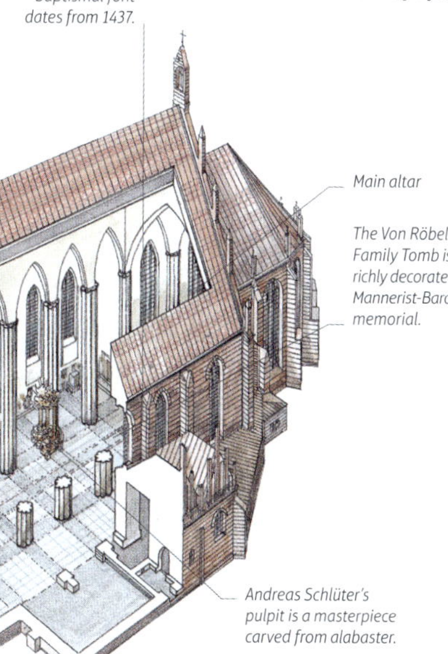

Marienkirche, a medieval parish church

Did You Know?

Home to the best organ music in the city, Marienkirche holds free concerts several times a week.

Crucifixion (1562), by Michael Rihenstein, depicts Christ flanked by Moses and St John the Baptist

EXPERIENCE MORE

Heiliggeistkapelle

W2 Spandauer Strasse 1 Hackescher Markt 100, 200, 300 M4, M5, M6

The Chapel of the Holy Spirit is the only surviving hospital chapel in Berlin. It was built as part of a hospital complex in the second half of the 13th century, and was rebuilt in the 15th century. The hospital was demolished in 1825, but the chapel was retained. In 1906, it was made into a newly erected College of Trade, designed by Cremer & Wolffenstein.

The chapel is a fine example of Brick Gothic construction. Its modest interior features a 15th-century star-shaped vault. The supports under the vault are decorated with half-statues of prophets and saints.

Marx-Engels-Forum

W3 Hackescher Markt, Alexanderplatz Rotes Rathaus 100, 200, 300

This vast square, which stretches from the Neptune fountain to the Spree river in the west, was given the inappropriate name Marx-Engels-Forum. Devoid of any surroundings, the only features in this square are the statues of Karl Marx and Friedrich Engels. The statues, added in 1986, are by Ludwig Engelhart.

The square is set to be developed into a new riverside park, complete with fountains and greenery. The statues of Marx and Engels will remain the centrepiece of the redeveloped square.

Did You Know?

Karl Marx studied at Berlin's Humboldt University and became a renowned Young Hegelian.

DDR Museum

W2 Karl-Liebknecht-Strasse 1 Hackescher Markt Museumsinsel 100, 245, 300 10am-8pm daily (to 10pm Sat) ddr-museum.de

This hands-on museum situated snugly on the

The larger-than-life-size statues of Marx (seated) and Engels at the Marx-Engels-Forum

Spree embankment opposite the Berliner Dom gives an insight into the daily lives of East Germans during the era of the DDR, and demonstrates how the secret police kept a watchful eye on the city's people. Exhibits on display here include a replica of a typical living room and a gleaming example of the iconic Trabant car.

Neptunbrunnen

X2 Spandauer Strasse (Rathausvorplatz) S & U Alexanderplatz, Rotes Rathaus S Hackescher Markt 100, 200

The magnificent Neptune Fountain, dating from 1895, is a Neo-Baroque-style feature on the square outside the Rotes Rathaus. It was moved to its present location from the former Stadtschloss (Berlin Castle) in 1969, and will return there when rebuilding of the castle is complete.

The statue of the Roman sea god Neptune in a dynamic pose at the centre of the fountain is surrounded by four figures representing Germany's greatest rivers: the Rhine, the Vistula, the Oder and the Elbe. The naturalism of the composition and the detail, such as the beautiful bronze fishes, crayfish and fishing nets, are noteworthy.

→ Tiered clock tower of the Rotes Rathaus

Rotes Rathaus

X3 Rathausstrasse 15 90 26 0 S Alexanderplatz U Rotes Rathaus, Klosterstrasse 100, 200, 248 9am-6pm Mon-Fri

This impressive structure is Berlin's main town hall; its name means "Red Town Hall". Its predecessor was a more modest building, and by the end of the 19th century it was insufficient to meet the needs of the growing metropolis.

The present building was designed by Hermann Friedrich Waesemann, and its construction was completed in 1869. The architect took his main inspiration from Italian Renaissance municipal buildings, but the tower is reminiscent of Laon cathedral in France. The walls are made from red brick and it was this, rather than the political orientation of the mayors, that gave the town hall its name. The building has a continuous frieze known as the "stone chronicle", which was added in 1879. It features scenes and figures from the city's history and the development of its economy and science.

The Rotes Rathaus was severely damaged during World War II and, following its reconstruction in the 1950s, it became the seat of the East Berlin authorities. The West Berlin magistrate was housed in the Schöneberg town hall. After the reunification of Germany in 1990, the Rotes Rathaus became the centre of authority, housing the offices of the mayor, the magistrates' offices and state rooms. The forecourt sculptures were added in 1958. These are by German sculptor Fritz Cremer and depict Berliners helping to rebuild the city.

Nikolaikirche

X3 Nikolaikirchplatz S & U Rotes Rathaus U Klosterstrasse 200, 248 10am-6pm daily stadtmuseum.de

The Nikolaikirche is the oldest sacred building of historic Berlin. The original structure erected on this site was started probably around 1230 when the town was granted its municipal rights. What remains now of this stone building is the massive base of the two-tower façade of the present church, which dates from c 1300. The presbytery was completed around 1402, but the construction of the main building went on until the mid-15th century. The result was a magnificent Gothic brick hall-church, featuring a chancel with an ambulatory and a row of low chapels. In 1877, Hermann Blankenstein, who conducted the church restoration works, removed most of its Baroque modifications and reconstructed the front towers.

Destroyed by bombing in 1945, the Nikolaikirche was eventually rebuilt in 1987 and shows a permanent exhibit on Berlin's history. The west wall of the southern nave contains Andreas Schlüter's monument to the goldsmith Daniel Männlich and his wife, which features a gilded relief portrait of the couple above a mock doorway.

Franziskaner Klosterkirche

N5 Klosterstrasse 74 U Klosterstrasse 248

These picturesque ruins surrounded by greenery are the remains of the early Gothic Franciscan Friary Church. The Franciscan friars settled in Berlin in the early 13th century. Between 1250 and 1265 they built a church and a friary, which survived almost unchanged until 1945. The church was a triple-nave basilica with an elongated presbytery, widening into a heptagonal section that was added to the structure in around 1300.

Protestants took over the church after the Reformation and the friary became a famous grammar school, whose graduates included Prussian Chancellor Otto von Bismarck. The friary was so damaged in World War II that it was subsequently demolished, while the church was partially reconstructed in 2003–4 and is now a venue for concerts and exhibitions. The giant Corinthian capitals, emerging from the grass

INSIDER TIP
Free Concerts

The Nikolaikirche hosts free 30-minute classical concerts every Friday at 5pm. Under the motto "Listen - Relax - Reflect" they span works from major composers as well as chamber music, and often employ the church's own organ.

←

The copper-clad double spires of the Nikolaikirche

near the church ruins, are from a portal from the Stadtschloss (City Palace).

Ephraim-Palais

X3 Poststrasse 16 S & U Rotes Rathaus U Klosterstrasse 200, 248 10am-6pm Tue-Sun stadtmuseum.de

The corner entrance of the Ephraim-Palais, standing at the junction of Poststrasse and Mühlendamm, used to be called *"die schönste Ecke Berlins"*, meaning "Berlin's most beautiful corner". This Baroque palace was built by Friedrich Wilhelm Dieterichs in 1766 for Nathan Veitel Heinrich Ephraim, Frederick the Great's Mint master and court jeweller. It remained in the possession of the Ephraim family until 1823, after which it changed hands several times.

During the widening of the Mühlendamm bridge in 1935 the palace was demolished, which may have been due in some part to the Jewish origin of its owner. Parts of the façade, saved from demolition, were stored in a warehouse in the western part of the city. In 1983 they were sent to East Berlin and used in the reconstruction of the palace, which was erected a few metres from its original site. One of the first-floor rooms features a restored Baroque ceiling, designed by Andreas Schlüter. The ceiling previously adorned Palais Wartenberg, which was dismantled in 1889.Currently, the Ephraim-Palais houses a branch of the Stadtmuseum Berlin (Berlin City Museum). It hosts a series of temporary exhibitions and events focused on Berlin's local artistic and cultural history. The palace is also home to the Ephraim Veitel Foundation for the Promotion of Jewish Life in Germany.

Knoblauchhaus

X3 Poststrasse 23 S & U Rotes Rathaus U Klosterstrasse 200, 248 10am-6pm Tue-Sun stadtmuseum.de

A small townhouse situated on elegant Poststrasse, the Knoblauchhaus is the only Baroque building in Nikolaiviertel that escaped damage during World War II. It was built in 1759 for the Knoblauch family, which includes the famous architect, Eduard Knoblauch. His works include, among others, the Neue Synagoge.

The current appearance of the building is the result of work carried out in 1835, when the façade was given a Neo-Classical look. The ground floor houses a popular wine bar, while the upper floors belong to a museum. On the first floor it is possible to see the interior of an early 19th-century middle-class home, including a beautiful Biedermeier-style room.

On the spiral staircase at Ephraim-Palais

Zille Museum

X3 Propststrasse 11 Klosterstrasse, Rotes Rathaus 200, 248 11am-6pm Mon-Sat, 1-6pm Sun zillemuseum-berlin.de

Artist, illustrator and photographer Heinrich Zille (1858–1929) was one of Berlin's best-known personalities. Renowned for his caricatures of everyday working-class life in the city, Zille was partly responsible for Berlin's image as a loud, rebellious, snarky, poor, proud and sometimes downright unsavoury capital.

Zille's collection of sketches, drawings, lithographs, photographs and cartoons can now be found in this small but charming three-room museum, along with a film and some family pictures. It has only minimal information in English, but the gist of the artist's work is easy to appreciate. His scabrously funny portrayals of beggars, urchins, labourers and prostitutes, finding in them a zest for life that transcended the poverty of their existence, made him immensely popular with Berlin's underclass.

Nearby you can find a reconstructed (and relocated) version of one of Zille's favourite watering holes, Zum Nussbaum, whose characters and stories often informed his work.

Parochialkirche

Y3 Klosterstrasse 67 24 75 95 10 Klosterstrasse 248 9am-3:30pm Mon-Fri

The Parish Church was, at one time, one of the most beautiful Baroque churches in Berlin. Johann Arnold Nering prepared the initial design, with four chapels framing a central tower. Unfortunately, Nering died as construction started in 1695. The work was continued by Martin Grünberg, but the collapse of the nearly completed vaults forced a change in the design. Instead of the intended tower over the main structure, a vestibule with a front tower was built. The church was completed in 1703, but then, in 1714, its tower was enlarged to accommodate a carillon.

World War II had a devastating effect on the Parochialkirche. The interior was completely destroyed, and the tower collapsed. Following stabilization of the main structure, the façade was restored, with reproduced historic elements set within a plain interior. In 2016, a replica of the former tower top was mounted. It bears a new carillon with 52 bells.

Stadtmauer

Y3 Waisenstrasse S & U Alexanderplatz Klosterstrasse 248

The Town Wall that once surrounded the settlements of Berlin and Cölln was erected in the second half of the 13th century. The ring of fortifications, built from brick and fieldstone, was made taller in the 14th century. Having finally lost its military significance by the 17th century, the wall was almost entirely dismantled, though some small sections survive around Waisenstrasse, having been incorporated into other buildings.

Gerichtslaube

X3 Poststrasse 28
241 56 97 S & U Rotes Rathaus 200, 248

This small building, with its sharply angled arcades, has had a turbulent history. It was built around 1280 as part of Berlin's old town hall in Spandauer Strasse. The original building was a single-storey arcaded construction with vaults supported by a central pillar. It was open on three sides and adjoined the shorter wall of the town hall. A further storey was added in 1485 to provide a hall, to which the magnificent lattice vaults were added several decades later, in 1555.

In 1692, Johann Arnold Nering refurbished the town hall in a Baroque style but left the arcades unaltered. Then, in 1868, the whole structure was dismantled to provide space for the new town hall, the Rotes Rathaus. The Baroque part was lost forever, but the Gothic arcades and the first-floor hall were moved to the palace gardens in Babelsberg, where they were reassembled as a building in their own right. When the Nikolaiviertel was undergoing renovation it was decided to restore the court of justice as well. The present building in Poststrasse is a copy of a part of the former town hall, erected on a different site from the original one. Inside it is a restaurant serving local cuisine.

Gaststätte Zur letzten Instanz by the Stadtmauer

Palais Schwerin and Münze

X3 Molkenmarkt 1-3
S & U Rotes Rathaus
U Klosterstrasse 248

These two adjoining houses have quite different histories. The older one, at Molkenmarkt No. 2, is Palais Schwerin, which was built by Jean de Bodt in 1704 for a government minister, Otto von Schwerin. Despite subsequent remodelling, the palace kept its beautiful sculpted window cornices, the interior wooden staircase and the magnificent cartouche featuring the von Schwerin family crest.

The adjoining house is the Münze, or Mint, built in 1936. Its façade is decorated with a copy of the frieze that once adorned the previous Neo-Classical Mint building in Werderscher Markt. The antique style of the frieze was designed by Friedrich Gilly and produced in the workshop of J G Schadow.

EAT

Zum Nussbaum

A reconstruction of a 16th-century pub, serving traditional Berlin cuisine including rollmops, meatballs and vegetable pancakes, as well as local beers.

X3 Am Nussbaum 3
242 30 95
Noon-10pm daily

Gaststätte Zur letzten Instanz

The oldest pub in Berlin has served everyone from Beethoven to Angela Merkel. The menu offers classic German fare, including pork knuckle and *Rinderroulade* (beef olive) in a classic wood-panelled room.

Y3
Waisenstrasse 14-16 Noon-1am Tue-Sat, noon-10pm Sun Mon
zurletzteninstanz.com

NORTH MITTE AND PRENZLAUER BERG

North of Torstrasse, Mitte begins to morph into the quieter, more residential district of Prenzlauer Berg. Characterized by its leafy, cobbled streets and refurbished *Altbaus* (19th-century tenements), it's one of the most gentrified and laid-back parts of the city. Relatively low on major sights, it offers instead a stream of pleasant cafés and restaurants, independent boutiques and cosy bars. That said, the Berlin Wall Memorial along Bernauer Strasse is a must for all history fans, and there are some interesting and unique museums scattered throughout the area.

↓ Tomb in Dorotheenstädtischer Friedhof

GEDENKSTÄTTE BERLINER MAUER

L2 Bernauer Strasse 119 Nordbahnhof Bernauer Strasse M8, M10 245, 247 Hours vary, check website berliner-mauer-gedenkstaette.de

28

The number of years that the Berlin Wall split the city in two.

The Berlin Wall Memorial on Bernauer Strasse is dedicated to the people who were killed by the Eastern border guards while attempting to escape into West Berlin.

Bernauer Strasse

Only small fragments of the Berlin Wall have survived. One of these, along Bernauer Strasse, is now an official place of remembrance. The location of the memorial here is poignant as the street was cut in two, resulting in people jumping to the West side from upper-floor buildings that stood right on the dividing line, while border guards were bricking up doors and windows facing west. Today, the memorial is a grim reminder of the hardship the division inflicted on the city. It includes a museum and various installations along 2 km (1 mile) of the former border.

↑ The Window of Remembrance shows those who died trying to cross the Wall

Structure of the Berlin Wall

Initially the Berlin Wall consisted simply of rolls of barbed wire. However, these were eventually replaced by a 4-m (13-ft) wall, safeguarded by a second wall made from reinforced concrete. This second wall was topped with a thick pipe to prevent people from gripping the top with their fingers. Along the Wall ran what was known as a "death zone", an area controlled by guards with dogs. Where the border passed close to houses, the inhabitants were relocated. Along the entire length of the 55-km (96-mile) wall there were 293 watchtowers, along with 57 bunkers and, later on, alarms.

GHOST STATIONS

Hidden inside Nordbahnhof station is a public exhibition about "ghost stations": stations where trains passed through East Germany but passengers were not able to leave the train until it reached West Berlin again. These stations were dimly lit places patrolled by East German guards and occasionally used for escapes.

HAMBURGER BAHNHOF

J3 Invalidenstrasse 50/51 S & U Hauptbahnhof 120, 147, 245, M41, M85 M5, M8, M10 10am-6pm Tue-Sun (to 8pm Thu) smb.museum

At the Museum of Contemporary Art, multimedia exhibits sit alongside exemplary pieces of modern art to help visitors understand the development of styles such as Pop Art and Expressionism.

This art museum is situated in a specially adapted Neo-Classical building that was originally constructed in 1847 as a railway station. Following extensive refurbishment by German architect Josef Paul Kleihues, it was finally opened to the public in 1996. At night, the façade is lit up by a neon light installation by American artist Dan Flavin. The museum has an ever-changing rotation of artworks by modern masters, including Beuys and Warhol, and more recent artists such as Kippenberger, Polke and Nauman. It also hosts a selection from the world-renowned Friedrich Christian Flick Collection of Art from the second half of the 20th century. Now, film, video, music and design sit alongside painting and sculpture, resulting in one of the best modern and contemporary art museums in Europe.

→ The Museum of Contemporary Art's Neo-Classical façade and garden

Did You Know?

The museum has works by German photographers such as Thomas Ruff and Andreas Gursky.

↑ Stark white interior of the museum's main gallery

→ *Volk Ding Zero* (2009), a 3-m- (9-ft-) high bronze sculpture by Georg Baselitz, was inspired by African, German and Polish folk art

GALLERY GUIDE

All works on display at the Hamburger Bahnhof are temporary and exhibits shown here may not necessarily be on display. The Rieckhallen shows selected works from the Friedrich Christian Flick Collection in rotation. The main hall is used for unusual installations and occasional fashion shows.

EXPERIENCE MORE

Brecht-Weigel-Museum

K3 Chausseestrasse 125 200 57 18 44 Naturkundemuseum, Oranienburger Tor 147, 245 12, M6 10am-3:30pm Tue & Sat, 10-11am Wed & Fri, 10am-6:30pm Thu, 11am-6pm Sun (with a tour guide)

The house where Bertolt Brecht and his wife, the actress Helene Weigel, lived and worked is now a memorial. Brecht, one of the greatest playwrights of the 20th century, was associated with Berlin from 1920, but emigrated in 1933. After the war, his left-wing views made him an attractive potential resident of the newly created German Socialist state. Lured by the promise of his own theatre, he returned to Berlin in 1948 with Weigel. He directed the Berliner Ensemble until his death, focusing mainly on productions of his own plays.

He lived in the first-floor apartment here from 1953 until he died in 1956. Weigel lived in the second-floor apartment, and after Brecht's death moved to the ground floor. She also founded an archive of Brecht's works, which is located on the second floor of the building.

Museum für Naturkunde

J3 Invalidenstrasse 43 Naturkunde museum 147, 245, M41, M85 M5, M8, M10 9:30am-6pm Tue-Fri; 10am-6pm Sat, Sun & public hols Mon museumfuernatur kunde.berlin

Berlin's Natural History Museum is one of the biggest in the world, with a massive collection numbering over 30 million exhibits. Occupying a beautiful Neo-Renaissance building completed in 1889, the museum has been operating for over a century, and despite several periods of extensive renovation, has maintained its old-fashioned atmosphere.

The most popular attractions at the museum include Europe's best-preserved *Tyrannosaurus rex* skeleton and the world's largest original dinosaur skeleton, which is housed in the glass-roofed courtyard. The colossal 23-m- (75-ft-) long and 12-m- (39-ft-) high skeleton of *Brachiosaurus brancai* was discovered in Tanzania in 1909 by a German fossil-hunting expedition. Six other smaller reconstructed dinosaur skeletons and a replica of the fossilized remains of an *Archaeopteryx lithographica*, thought to be the prehistoric link between reptiles and birds, complete this fascinating display.

The adjacent rooms feature countless colourful shells and butterflies, as well as a sizeable selection of taxidermy. Particularly popular are the dioramas – scenes of mounted animals set against the background of their natural habitat. There is also a significant collection of minerals and meteorites.

MAX REINHARDT (1873-1943)

This actor and director became famous as one of the 20th century's greatest theatre reformers. He worked in Berlin, first as an actor in the Deutsches Theater, and then from 1905 as its director. As well as setting up the Kammerspiele, he produced plays for the Neues Theater am Schiffbauerdamm (renamed the Berliner Ensemble) and the Schumann Circus (later to become the Friedrichstadtpalast). His experimental productions of classic and modern works brought him worldwide fame. Forced to emigrate because of his Jewish origins, he left Germany in 1933 for the United States, where he died in 1943.

Deutsches Theater

K4 Schumann-strasse 13A 28 44 10 S & U Friedrichstrasse U Oranienburger Tor 147 12, M1 deutschestheater.de

This theatre building first opened in 1850 as the Friedrich-Wilhelm Städtisches Theater, and in 1883, following reconstruction, it was renamed Deutsches Theater. It was here that Max Reinhardt began his career as an actor, before becoming director from 1905 until 1933.

Another famous figure associated with the theatre was Bertolt Brecht who, until 1933, wrote plays for it; after World War II he became the director of the Berliner Ensemble, whose first venue was here at the Deutsches Theater.

↑ Dorotheenstädtischer Friedhof memorial to Johann Gottlieb Fichte

Dorotheen-städtischer Friedhof

K3 Chausseestrasse 126 461 72 79 U Naturkundemuseum, Oranienburger Tor 142, 245, 247 12, M6, M8, 8am-sunset daily

This small cemetery, established in 1763, is the final resting place of many famous Berlin citizens, including Bertolt Brecht and Helene Weigel. Many of the monuments are outstanding works of art, coming from the workshops of prominent Berlin architects, including Karl Friedrich Schinkel and Johann Gottfried Schadow, who are both buried here. A tranquil, tree-filled oasis, the cemetery is reached via a narrow path, leading from the street between the wall of the French Cemetery and the Brecht-Weigel-Museum.

Volksbühne

N3 Rosa-Luxemburg-Platz 24 06 55 U Rosa-Luxemburg-Platz 100, 142, 200 M8

Founded during the early years of the 20th century, the People's Theatre owes its existence to the efforts of the 100,000 members of the Freie Volksbühne (Free People's Theatre Society). The original theatre was built in 1913, a time when the Scheunen-viertel district was under-going rapid redevelopment. During the 1920s the theatre became famous thanks to the director Erwin Piscator (1893–1966), who later achieved great acclaim at the Metropol-Theater on Nollendorfplatz.

Destroyed during World War II, the theatre was rebuilt in the early 1950s to a design by Hans Richter. Now one of the city's most important cultural spots, it often stages contro-versial performances.

Berliner Ensemble

K4 Bertolt-Brecht-Platz 1 28 40 81 55 S & U Friedrichstrasse 147 12, M1

Designed by Heinrich Seeling and completed in 1892, this theatre has seen many changes in Berlin's cultural life. First known as the Neues Theater am Schiffbauerdamm, it soon became famous for staging important premieres and for its memorable productions by Max Reinhardt. These included Shakespeare's *A Midsummer Night's Dream* in 1905, which, for the first time, used a revolving stage and real trees as part of the set. In 1928 the theatre presented the world premiere of Bertolt Brecht's *The Threepenny Opera*. The building was destroyed during World War II and subsequently restored with a much simpler exterior, but its Neo-Baroque interior survived intact.

The theatre returned to prominence in 1954 with the arrival of the Berliner Ensemble under the directorship of Brecht and his wife, actress Helene Weigel. The move from its former home, the Deutsches Theater, to the new venue was celebrated by staging the world premiere of Brecht's *The Caucasian Chalk Circle*. After Brecht's death, Weigel took over the running of the theatre, maintaining its innovative tradition.

Oranienburger Strasse

K3 S Oranienburger Strasse, Hackescher Markt U Oranienburger Tor 12, M1, M4, M5, M6

Oranienburger Strasse is home to numerous cafés, restaurants, bars and clubs. The district has traditionally been a centre for alternative culture, and was home to the famous state-sponsored Tacheles centre for the arts, which was previously occupied by artist squatters. The Tacheles centre has since closed, but its legacy lives on, with several excellent art galleries operating in this area. As you stroll around Oranienburger Strasse and the neighbourhood, it is worth looking out for a number of interesting buildings, such as the one at Oranienburger Strasse No. 71–2, built by Christian Friedrich Becherer in 1789 for Germany's Great National Masonic Lodge.

Friedrichstadt-palast

K4 Friedrichstrasse 107 S Oranienburger Strasse, Friedrichstrasse U Oranienburger Tor 147 12, M1 W palast.berlin

Multicoloured glass tiles and a pink, plume-shaped neon sign make up the eye-catching façade of the Friedrichstadt Palace. Built in the early 1980s, this massive theatre complex specializes in spectacular,

→ Samuel Beckett's *Endgame*, staged by the Berliner Ensemble

↑ Michel Majerus on show at the Sammlung Boros

Vegas-style shows involving gigantic casts and expensive special effects. Nearly 2,000 seats are arranged around a huge podium, used by turns as a circus arena, a swimming pool and an ice rink. A further huge stage is equipped with every technical facility. There is also a small cabaret theatre with seats for 240 spectators.

The original and much-loved Friedrichstadtpalast suffered bomb damage during World War II and was replaced with the existing version. Built as a market hall, the earlier building was later used as a circus ring. In 1918, it became the Grosse Schauspielhaus, or Grand Playhouse, opening in 1919 with a memorable production of Aeschylus's *The Oresteia*, directed by Max Reinhardt. The old building was extraordinary, its central dome supported by a forest of columns and topped with Expressionist, stalactite-like decoration. An equally fantastical interior provided seating for 5,000 spectators.

Sammlung Boros

K4 Reinhardtstrasse 20 S & U Oranienburger Tor 147 M1, M12 3-8pm Thu, 10am-8pm Fri-Sun sammlung-boros.de

This former air-raid bunker, built by architect Karl Bonatz, is an intriguing gallery location. The bunker has a chequered history; once used as a POW prison by the Red Army, it later became a warehouse, then in the 1990s it was a popular club. In 2003, art collector Christian Boros bought the building and converted it into a gallery space. It houses the Boros Collection of modern art. No more than 12 guests can visit at one time and advance online registration is required.

DRINK

Buck & Breck

This hipster bar is cunningly disguised as an art gallery. If you can find it, and if there are seats going spare, you'll be rewarded with impeccable drinks.

M2 Brunnenstrasse 177 Hours vary, check website buckandbreck.com

---

Becketts Kopf

Find the wrinkled visage of Mr Beckett staring from a dark window, ring the bell and enter Prenzlauer Berg's best cocktail spot.

N1 Pappelallee 64 8pm-2am Wed-Sat beckets-kopf.de

Sophienkirche

M3 Grosse Hamburger Strasse 31 308 79 20 Hackescher Markt Weinmeisterstrasse M1, M4, M5, M6 1-6pm Mon-Sat

A narrow passageway and a wrought-iron gate take you through to this small Baroque church. Founded in 1712 by Queen Sophia Luisa, the wife of Frederick I of Prussia, this was the first parish church of the newly developed Spandauer Vorstadt area, which had been growing steadily since the Middle Ages. Johann Friedrich Grael designed the tower, which was built between 1729 and 1735. In 1892 the building was extended to include a presbytery, though the church still retains its original Baroque character. A modest, rectangular structure, Sophienkirche is typical of its period, with the tower adjoining the narrower side elevation. The interior still contains a number of its original 18th-century furnishings, including the pulpit and the font. Several gravestones dating from the 18th century have survived in the small graveyard surrounding the church.

Monbijoupark

L4 Oranienburger Strasse Oranienburger Strasse, Hackescher Markt M1, M4, M5, M6

Little Monbijou ("My Jewel") Park, between Oranienburger Strasse and the Spree river, was once the grounds of the Monbijou Palace. Damaged by bombing during World War II, the ruined palace was dismantled in 1960.

A rare green space in this part of the city, the well-kept park is a pleasant place to relax. It features a marble bust of the poet Adelbert von Chamisso, and there is also an open-air swimming pool for children.

Neue Synagoge and Centrum Judaicum

L4 Oranienburger Strasse 28-30 Oranienburger Strasse M1, M5 Hours vary, check website Jewish hols centrumjudaicum.de

The New Synagogue, by architect Eduard Knoblauch, was completed in 1866. It was the largest synagogue in Germany at the time. The design, a highly sophisticated response to the asymmetrical shape of the plot of land, used a narrow façade flanked by a pair of towers and crowned with a dome containing a round vestibule. Small rooms opened off the vestibule, including an anteroom and two prayer rooms – one large and one small. The two towers opened onto a staircase leading to the galleries,

MOSES MENDELSSOHN (1729-86)

One of the greatest German philosophers of the 18th century, Moses Mendelssohn arrived in Berlin in 1743 and was a central figure in the Jewish struggle for citizenship rights. About 50 years later, the first Jewish family was granted full civic rights; however, it was not until the Emancipation Edict of 1812 that Jewish men finally became full citizens. The grandfather of composer Felix Mendelssohn-Bartholdy, he is immortalized in the drama *Nathan der Weise* (Nathan the Wise) by his friend Gotthold Ephraim Lessing.

←

Triple domes of the Neue Synagoge

and the main hall had space for around 3,000 worshippers. An innovative use of iron in the construction of the roof and galleries put the synagogue at the forefront of 19th-century civil engineering. This fascinating structure was Berlin's largest synagogue until the night of 9–10 November 1938, when it was partially destroyed in the course of the infamous Kristallnacht (Night of Broken Glass), when thousands of synagogues, cemeteries, Jewish homes and shops were looted and burned by soldiers and Nazi supporters. The building was damaged further by Allied bombing in 1943 and was finally demolished in 1958 by government authorities. Reconstruction began in 1988 and the stunning new building was completed in 1995.

Adjoining the New Synagoge, the Centrum Judaicum (Jewish Centre) occupies the former premises of the Jewish community council, and contains a library, archives and a research centre devoted to the history and cultural heritage of the Jewish people of Berlin. The Centre also uses restored rooms of the Neue Synagoge to exhibit materials relating to the local Jewish community, which includes information on the famed Jewish thinker and social activist, Moses Mendelssohn.

Be aware that security is strict at both the Synagoge and the Centrum Judaicum.

Hackesche Höfe

M4 Rosenthaler Strasse 40-41
Hackescher Markt
Weinmeisterstrasse
M1, M4, M5, M6

Running from Oranienburger Strasse and Rosenthaler up as far as Sophienstrasse, the Hackesche Höfe (*Höfe* means "courtyards") is a huge, early 20th-century complex that attracts more than a million visitors every year. It is made up of an intricate series of nine interconnecting courtyards surrounded by tall and beautifully proportioned buildings. The development dates from 1906, and was designed by Kurt Berendt and August Endell, both of whom were outstanding exponents of the German Secession style.

Damaged during World War II, Hackesche Höfe has been restored to its original splendour. The first courtyard is especially attractive, featuring glazed facings with geometric designs decorated in fabulous colours. A whole range of restaurants, bars, art galleries, shops and restaurants can be found here, as well as offices and apartments on the upper floors. The complex also has a small theatre, the Chamäleon, specializing in contemporary circus shows. For many Berliners the Hackesche Höfe has become something of a cult spot, and for visitors it is definitely a sight not to be missed.

Kollwitzplatz

N2 Senefelderplatz

This green square is named after the German artist Käthe Kollwitz, who once lived nearby. It was here that the socially engaged painter and sculptor observed and painted the daily hardships of the working-class people living in overcrowded tenements. One of her sculptures stands on the square, now the social hub of the district, with a Thursday organic farmers' market, cool bars, restaurants and shops that extend into the surrounding streets. Käthe Kollwitz's work can be seen at the Käthe-Kollwitz-Museum.

Zionskirche

M2 Zionskirchplatz 449 21 91 Senefelderplatz, Rosenthaler Platz 12, M1 Hours vary, call ahead

Located in the square named after it, Zionskirchplatz, this Protestant church was built between 1866 and 1873 – a tranquil oasis in the middle of this lively district. Both the square and the church have always been centres of political opposition. During the Third Reich, resistance groups against the Nazi regime congregated at the church, and when the Communists were in power in East Germany, the alternative "environment library" (an information and documentation centre) was established here. Church and other opposition groups active here played a decisive role in the transformation of East Germany in 1989–90.

↑ Soaring tower of the Neo-Romantic Zionskirche

Alte and Neue Schönhauser Strasse

N3 Hackescher Markt Weinmeisterstrasse M1

Alte Schönhauser Strasse is one of the oldest streets in the Spandauer Vorstadt district, running from the centre of Berlin to Pankow and Schönhausen. In the 18th and 19th centuries this was a popular residential area among wealthy merchants.

During World War II, however, its proximity to the neighbouring Jewish district of Scheunenviertel, devastated by the Nazis, decreased its popularity considerably. For a long time, bars, small factories, workshops and retail shops were the hallmark of this neighbourhood. Small private shops survived longer here than in most parts of Berlin, and the largely original houses maintained much of their pre-1939 atmosphere. Much has changed, however, since the fall of the Berlin Wall. Some of the houses have been restored, and many old businesses have been replaced by fashionable shops, restaurants and bars, making it one of the most expensive retail areas in the city. Throughout the district, the old and the new now stand side by side. One poignant example is at Neue Schönhauser Strasse No. 14. This interesting old house in the German Neo-Renaissance style was built in 1891 to a design by Alfred Messel. The first-floor rooms were home to the first public reading room in Berlin, while on the ground floor was a *Volkskaffeehaus*, a soup kitchen, with separate rooms for men and women. Here the poor of the neighbourhood could get a free bowl of soup and a cup of ersatz (imitation) coffee.

Gedenkstätte Grosse Hamburger Strasse

M4 Grosse Hamburger Strasse Hackescher Markt 12, M1, M4, M5, M6

An otherworldly group of figures in bronze stands on Grosse Hamburger Strasse, bearing witness to the extermination of the street's Jewish community. On this spot once stood a Jewish home for the elderly which, during World War II, served as a detention centre for thousands of Jewish people who were condemned to death in the camps at Auschwitz and Theresienstadt.

Until the years leading up to World War II, Grosse Hamburger Strasse was one of the main streets of Berlin's Jewish quarter. It was home to several Jewish schools, the old-people's home and the city's oldest Jewish cemetery, established in 1672 and in use until 1827.

At No. 27 stands a Jewish school founded in 1778 by Moses Mendelssohn. Rebuilt in 1906, the building was reopened as a Jewish secondary school in 1993. The empty space once occupied by house No.15–16, destroyed by World War II bombing, is now an installation, *The Missing House* by Christian Boltanski, with plaques recording the names and professions of the former inhabitants of the house.

EAT

Yam Yam

Popular with local fashionistas, this canteen-style restaurant uses organic Korean vegetables and hot spices for owner Sumi Ha's *cha chang myun* and *bibimbap*.

M3 Alte Schönhauser Strasse 6 Noon-11pm Tue-Sat, 5-11pm Sun yamyam-berlin.de

Night Kitchen

This cosy spot serves up personalized Israeli- and Mediterranean-inspired small plates. If it's sunny, grab a seat in the pretty light-strung garden.

L3 Oranienburger Strasse 32 5pm-midnight Tue-Sun nightkitchenberlin.com

Rutz

A star in Berlin's gourmet scene, Rutz is a Michelin-starred venue offering dishes based on local recipes served with a creative twist.

K3 Chaussee strasse 8 Hours vary, see website rutz-restaurant.de

Metzer Eck

In its heyday, this traditional restaurant was a meeting point for Prenzlauer Berg's GDR bohemian luminaries. It still has oodles of character and serves cheap, simple dishes like meatballs and *Bockwurst*.

N2 Metzer Strasse 33 4pm-1am Mon-Fri, 6pm-1am Sat metzer-eck.de

Café Cinema, a legendary bohemian meeting place in Haus Schwarzenburg

Haus Schwarzenberg Museums

M4 Rosenthaler Strasse 39 Hackesher Markt Weinmeister-strasse N2, N5, N42 M1, M5 haus-schwarzenberg.org

The Haus Schwarzenberg complex is a cool and grungy hangover from the early 1990s. Its crumbling, postwar façades are splattered with colourful street art – some by famous local artists like El Bocho and Miss Van. Its courtyard consciously eschews high-end boutiques and cafés i n favour of an edgy bar, a street-art shop and gallery and the Monsterkabinett: a collection of moving mechanical monsters built by the owners, a nonprofit artist collective. The complex also hosts two notable, small museums that explore local resistance to the Nazis. The Museum Blindenwerkstatt Otto Weidt (Museum Otto Weidt's Workshop for the Blind) tells the story of Otto Weidt, a German entrepreneur who saved a number of his blind Jewish employees from the Nazis. It displays photographs and back-stories of Weidt, his family and his workers, and visitors can still see the room where Jewish families were hidden. The second museum, the engaging Anne-Frank-Zentrum, looks into the famous diarist's life.

Torstrasse

M3 Oranienburger Tor, Rosenthaler Platz, Rosa-Luxemburg-Platz 142 M1, M8

Formerly a customs road and Berlin's northern border around 1800, Torstrasse is now a main thoroughfare connecting Prenzlauer Allee and Friedrichstrasse. Once a largely working-class bohemian area, it has become fairly urbanized today. The 19th-century residential buildings lining the street have been gentrified to make way for cool bars, trendy cafés, gourmet restaurants, art galleries and fashion shops. "Soto", the area south of Torstrasse, has the highest number of independent designers and brand outfitters in the city.

Jüdischer Friedhof

N2 Schönhauser Allee 22-25 441 98 24 Senefelderplatz 8am-4pm Mon-Thu, 7:30am-1pm Fri Sat, Sun & public hols

This small Jewish Cemetery is hidden behind thick walls on Schönhauser Allee, but the serene atmosphere, with tall trees and thick undergrowth, is a welcome oasis. The cemetery was laid out in 1827, though the oldest gravestone dates back to the 14th century. It was Berlin's second-largest Jewish cemetery after the Jüdischer Friedhof Weissensee.

Among the many prominent Berliners resting here are the painter Max Liebermann; Giacomo Meyerbeer, the composer and musical director of the Staatsoper Unter den Linden; and the author David Friedländer (1750–1834). The lapidarium, built in 2005, displays rescued gravestones from this and other historic Jewish cemeteries in Berlin.

Sophienstrasse

M3 Hackescher Markt Weinmeisterstrasse M1, M4, M5, M6

The area around Sophienstrasse and Gipsstrasse was first settled at the end of the 17th century. In fact, Sophientrasse was once the main street of Spandauer Vorstadt. The area underwent extensive restoration during the 1980s that was designed to preserve its small-town character. Today, the narrow lanes and three-storey buildings are reminiscent of Prague's Old Town. It was one of the first parts of East Berlin in which renovation was chosen over large-scale demolition and redevelopment. Now these modest but charming 18th-century Neo-Classical buildings are home to different arts and crafts workshops, cosy bars, a puppet theatre, unusual boutiques and interesting art galleries.

One building with a particularly eventful history is Sophienstrasse No. 18. Erected in 1852, the house was remodelled in 1904 on behalf of the Craftsmen's Association, an educational society for blue-collar workers, to serve as their headquarters (Handwerkervereinshaus). The hall in the yard (Sophiensaele) was used as a meeting venue by revolutionary leftists like Rosa Luxemburg and Karl Liebknecht in the 1920s.

The main door of Sophienstrasse No. 21 leads into a row of interior courtyards running up as far as Gipsstrasse.

TOP 5 SHOPPING AREAS IN DOWNTOWN MITTE

Hackescher Höfe
Renovated Art Nouveau shopping complex.

Alte Schönhauser Strasse
Extension of Schönhauser Allee.

Neue Schönhauser Strasse
Small street packed with a number of boutiques, cafés and restaurants.

Mulackstrasse
Elegant side street, home to many local design stores.

Steinstrasse
Parallel to Mulackstrasse, with many shops and cafés.

↑ Colourful façade of the Handwerkervereinshaus

Synagoge Rykestrasse

O2 Rykestrasse 53 88 02 81 47 Senefelderplatz

This synagogue is one of the few reminders of old Jewish life in Berlin, and one of the few in Germany left almost intact during the Nazi regime. Built in 1904, the red-brick synagogue has a basilica-like nave with three aisles and certain Moorish features. Due to its location inside a huge tenement area, Nazi SA troops did not set it on fire during the Kristallnacht pogrom on 9 November 1938, when hundreds of other synagogues were razed to the ground. The synagogue welcomes visitors to its public services.

Prater

N1 Kastanienallee 7-9 448 56 88 Eberswalder Strasse 12, M1

Prater has been one of Berlin's best-known entertainment institutions for more than a century. The building, along with its quiet courtyard, was constructed in the 1840s and later became the city's oldest and largest beer garden. It now houses a restaurant, serving Berlin specialities, and stages a variety of pop, rock and folk concerts and theatre shows.

Did You Know?

The periphery of the cemetery is reserved for the upper classes; the overgrown centre for the less well off.

Alter Jüdischer Friedhof

M4 Grosse Hamburger Strasse Hackescher Markt M1

The Old Jewish Cemetery was established in 1672 and, until 1827 when it was finally declared full, it provided the resting place for over 12,000 Berliners. After this date, Jewish people were buried in cemeteries in Schönhauser Allee and in Herbert-Baum-Strasse. The Alter Jüdischer Friedhof was destroyed by the Nazis in 1943, and in 1945 the site was turned into a park. Embedded in the original cemetery wall, a handful of Baroque *masebas* (or tombstones) continue to recall the past. A *maseba* stands on the grave of the philosopher Moses Mendelssohn, erected in 1990 by members of the Jewish community.

Wasserturm

O2 Knaackstrasse/ Belforter Strasse Senefelderplatz

The unofficial symbol of this district is a giant 30-m- (100-ft-) high

water tower, standing high on Windmühlenberg (wind-mill hill) in the heart of Prenzlauer Berg. It was here that some of the windmills, once typical in Prenzlauer Berg, produced flour for the city's population.

The distinctive brick water tower was built in 1874 by Wilhelm Vollhering and served as a reservoir for the country's first running water system. In the 1930s, the basement served as a makeshift jail, where Nazi SA troops held and tortured Communist opponents. This dark period is marked by a plaque.

Leafy avenue in the Alter Jüdischer Friedhof

The Wasserturm, with its brickwork cladding

Kulturbrauerei

N1 Schönhauser Allee 36-39 Eberswalder Strasse 12, M1, M10 10am-6pm Tue-Sun (to 8pm Thu) hdg.de

This vast Neo-Gothic, industrial red-and-yellow-brick building was once Berlin's most famous brewery, Schultheiss, built by the architect Franz Schwechten in 1889–92. Now housing the Kulturbrauerei (culture brewery), the massive complex with a number of courtyards has been revived as a cultural and entertainment centre, with concert venues, restaurants and cafés, and a cinema, as well as artists' ateliers. A popular Christmas market is also held here in December.

Inside the Kulturbrauerei, the Museum Alltagsgeschichte der DDR (Museum of Everyday Life in the GDR) features both permanent and temporary exhibitions on the former East Germany. Don't miss the reconstructed flat, or the "Trabi-Tent", a typically ingenious East German solution to a caravan holiday with no caravan.

SHOP

Goldhahn und Sampson

This gourmet food store stocks high-end, high-quality products and a good selection of cookbooks.

O1 Dunckerstrasse 9 8am-8pm Mon-Sat goldhahnundsampson.de

Thatchers

A popular women's clothing store, Thatchers sells dresses, skirts and accessories.

N1 Kastanienallee 21 11am-7pm Mon-Sat thatchers.de

Saint George's English Bookshop

Book lovers will relish the range of popular literature sold here.

O2 Wörther Strasse 27 11am-8pm Mon-Fri, 11am-7pm Sat saintgeorgesbookshop.com

FRIEDRICHSHAIN

Once home to political anarchists, Friedrichshain has largely lost its radical left-wing image in favour of a more cosmopolitan air – especially around the central Boxhagener Platz, which is studded with buzzing cafés and restaurants, edgy bars and indie boutiques. The district is also popular for nightlife, and its Volkspark is one of the city's most popular recreational spots.

↓ Colourful graffiti on the Berlin Wall

The tree-lined boulevard stretches from Frankfurter Tor to Strausberger Platz

KARL-MARX-ALLEE

P5

The area around this 2-km (1-mile) boulevard has a vibrant and relaxed atmosphere. Most residents are in their mid-twenties, drawn here by the alternative cafés and cool bars.

The route leading east to Poland and Moscow was initially called Frankfurter Strasse, and then renamed Stalinallee in 1949. Having suffered severe damage during World War II, the street was chosen as the site for the construction showpiece of the new German Democratic Republic, featuring spacious and luxurious apartments for workers, as well as commercial infrastructure.

The avenue was widened to 90 m (300 ft) and, in the course of the next 10 years, huge residential tower blocks and a row of shops were built on it. The first houses to be built on the street were Modernist in style and quickly denounced as "too Western". They were hidden behind trees while the rest of the street proceeded in a more aptly Socialist style. The next architects followed a style known in the Soviet Union as "pastry chef", which was "nationalistic in form, but socialist in content", and linked the whole work to Berlin's own traditions. Hence there are motifs taken from famous Berlin architects Schinkel and Gontard, as well as from the renowned Meissen porcelain.

The buildings on this street, renamed Karl-Marx-Allee in 1961, are now considered historic monuments, and the section between Strausberger Platz and Frankfurter Tor is effectively a huge open-air museum of Socialist Realist architecture. The buildings have been cleaned up and the crumbling details are gradually being restored.

WORKER UPRISING

In 1953, Karl-Marx-Allee was the site of a mass worker uprising. Increasing food costs and work quotas led people to begin peaceful protests, which were followed by strikes and marches as their calls fell on deaf ears. The situation escalated, with the uprising spreading across East Germany. The uprising ended on 17 June, when Soviet tanks were called in to help the police suppress a protest in East Berlin. Over 50 workers were killed and many more injured in the revolt.

EXPERIENCE MORE

Peres Projects

P5 Karl-Marx-Allee 82 Weberwiese, Straussberger Platz 142, N5 11am-6pm Mon-Fri peresprojects.com

This well-known art gallery is the latest of a series of venues – a typically box-shaped room with concrete columns, large, street-facing windows and pristine white-painted walls. Known for championing artists early in their careers as well as the occasional established name, it shows consistently innovative works from international contemporary figures ranging from North American artists like James Franco and Brent Wadden to locals such as the German painter David Ostrowski.

Volkspark Friedrichshain

P3 Am Friedrichshain/Friedenstrasse 142, 200 M5, M6, M8, M10

The extensive park complex of Friedrichshain, with its picturesque nooks and crannies, was one of Berlin's first public parks. It was laid out in the 1840s on the basis of a design by landscape architect Peter Joseph Lenné, with the idea of creating an alternative Tiergarten for the eastern districts of the city. The greatest attraction here is the Fountain of Fairy Tales (or Märchenbrunnen) by Ludwig Hoffmann, built in 1902–13. It is a spectacular feature in a Neo-Baroque style, its fountain pools decorated with small statues of turtles and other animals. The fountain is surrounded by well-known characters from the fairy tales by the Brothers Grimm. There's a sports and games area and a challenging outdoor climbing wall. Trails cross over Mont Klamott, an artificial hill constructed from the rubble of buildings destroyed in World War II.

↑ Bust of Frederick the Great in Volkspark Friedrichshain

Computerspiele-museum

P5 Karl-Marx-Allee 93a Weberwiese, Straussberger Platz 347, N5 10am-8pm daily computerspielemuseum.de

The Computer Games Museum is Europe's first museum for video and computer games. It displays over 300 items from a life-size Lara Croft to a Wall of Hardware with vintage games and toys. Here also is pretty much every arcade machine and games console ever made, including the immense but pioneering Nimrod from 1951, and the Brown Box from 1959, developed by Ralph H Baer – the inventor of video games for home use. There's also a small penny arcade (no payment required) with vintage slot machine games like Donkey Kong, Asteroids and Space Invaders, and more contemporary game systems like the 3D PlayStation monitor from Sony.

Kino International

O4 Karl-Marx-Allee 33 S & U Alexanderplatz U Schillingstrasse N5 kino-international.com

One of the most eye-catching buildings on the Karl-Marx-Allee, this large, blocky and historic cinema was a landmark in the GDR

Browsing wares at Boxhagener Platz's weekend market

and remains so today – not least for its cameo role in the classic movie *Goodbye Lenin* and, since 1995, its UNESCO-heritage status. Used for hosting premieres until the fall of the Wall, it still operates as a cinema, with state-of-the-art facilities and a good rotation of commercial and arthouse movies. It's worth taking a moment to inspect the sandstone reliefs on the outside as well as the distinctly retro-looking foyer.

Boxhagener Platz

R6 S & U Frankfurter Allee U Frankfurter Tor 240, N40 M5, M10, M13, 21

The most famous square in Friedrichshain, Boxhagener Platz (locally known as "Boxi") serves as both a historical centre point for the area and a social hub. Named after the former nearby manor farm and hamlet of Boxhagen, these days it's surrounded by shops, bars, galleries and restaurants that draw a real mix of Berliners. At weekends Boxi is especially popular due to its excellent markets. The Saturday food market has been held here since 1903 and offers an array of fruit and vegetables, but also food stalls selling everything from falafel to grilled fish. And at the Sunday flea market you can find a variety of items such as jewellery and vinyl and second-hand clothes.

The streets leading off from the square – Grünberger Strasse, Krossener Strasse, Gärtnerstrasse and Gabriel-Max-Strasse – are also worth exploring for their cafés, boutiques, restaurants and bars, while nearby Simon-Dach-Strasse and RAW Gelände are well known for their upbeat weekend nightlife.

The most famous square in Friedrichshain, Boxhagener Platz (locally known as "Boxi") serves as both a historical centre point for the area and a social hub.

EAT

Schneeweiss

One of Friedrichshain's few upmarket restaurants, "Snow White" combines a minimalist aesthetic with an Alpine menu that straddles Italian, Austrian and south German dishes: think *Wiener schnitzel* and Bavarian pasta.

R6 Simplonstrasse 16 5-10pm Mon-Sat, 10am-3pm & 5-10pm Sun schneeweiss-berlin.de

East Side Gallery

P7 Mühlenstrasse S & U Warschauer Strasse S Ostbahnhof 24, 140, 300 M10 W eastsidegallery-berlin.com

Running alongside the River Spree, the East Side Gallery is the longest surviving stretch of the Berlin Wall – as well as the most colourful, thanks to the numerous paintings that have adorned its surface since 1990. More than 100 artists have contributed to the gallery, and millions of visitors to the city come here every year to enjoy their work.

Although it's not the city's official Berlin Wall memorial, this 1.3-km (0.8-mile) stretch is the longest section of the Wall that still exists today. Located in the former East Berlin district of Friedrichshain, the Wall was protected by border guards and watchtowers until the collapse of the GDR in 1989. Soon after, dozens of artists began using it as a political canvas, decorating it with murals, slogans and paintings. The improvised gallery was appointed an official one in 1990 and given protected memorial status the following year. The gallery was repainted for its 20th anniversary in 2009, with some original artists refusing to repaint or retouch their artworks for reasons of authenticity. In 2016, a multimedia museum opened at the south end of the East Side Gallery, giving an overview of the Berlin Wall era through screens,

The graffiti-covered East Side Gallery, bringing back memories of the Wall era

interactive displays, original newsreel footage and filmed interviews with Berliners who lived through it.

Oberbaumbrücke

Q7 S & U Warschauer Strasse U Schlesisches Tor 300, 347 M10

A popular Berlin landmark, this pretty bridge crossing the Spree river was built in 1896 to a design by Otto Stahn. It is made from reinforced concrete, but the arches are faced with red brick. The central arch is marked by a pair of crenellated Neo-Gothic towers. The most decorative element of the bridge, a Neo-Gothic arcade, supports a line of the U-Bahn.

Prior to reunification, the bridge linked districts from opposing sides of the Wall, and only pedestrians with the correct papers were able to cross. It is now open to traffic.

RAW Gelände

Q7 Revaler Strasse 99 S & U Warschauer Strasse 347 M5, M10, M13

Formerly a 19th-century repair yard owned by the national railway (its official name was "Reichsbahn-Ausbesserungs-Werk", hence RAW), this sprawling complex of graffiti-spattered warehouses and buildings today represents one of the most prominent alternative cultural spaces in the city. It's fun to stroll around any time, especially if you're a street-art fan, though it really comes alive in the evenings at weekends. The 7-ha (17.5-acre) site incorporates a slew of clubs and bars, a couple of places to eat, an indoor skate hall and a climbing wall that was once a World War II bunker. Haubentaucher is a trendy event and concert venue with an outdoor pool and beer garden for the warmer months.

One of the most exciting enterprises here is Urban Spree, a masterpiece in post-apocalyptic urban styling. The 1,700-sq-m (18,000-sq-ft) space is devoted to "urban cultures", notably street and graphic art, via a rotating procession of artist residencies, exhibitions, workshops and concerts. Its art shows include high-profile local and international street artists who often paint the entire compound.

BERGHAIN

Often voted the best techno club in the world, this former power station features a cavernous main room, the smaller Panorama Bar upstairs and an experimental music area on the ground floor. Its minimal, industrial design aesthetic is as uncompromising as the notorious door policy - but if you can get in, expect some of the best DJs playing all through the weekend. Weekday concerts tend to be ticket-only and much easier to get into; check website for more details *(berghain.de)*

TIERGARTEN

At the heart of the city, Berlin's central park bursts to life with gardens, meadows and lakes threaded together with pleasant pathways. The wide boulevard Strasse des 17 Juni divides the park through the centre. Its southern fringe borders the bustling areas of Potsdamer Platz and the Kulturforum, while the northern edge runs parallel to important sights like the Reichstag and Regierungsviertel.

↓ Inside the Reichstag dome designed by Norman Foster

The historic Reichstag topped with a modern glass dome

REICHSTAG

J5 Platz der Republik Brandenburger Tor Bundestag 100, 245, M85 8am-midnight daily; bookings for a time slot to visit or for a restaurant reservation are required at least a few days in advance bundestag.de

One of Berlin's most recognizable landmarks, the Reichstag, seat of Germany's parliament, has survived fascism, fire, bombardment and being wrapped in fireproof polypropylene fabric by artists to become a symbol of a modern, politically transparent Germany.

EAT

Dachgarten-Restaurant

The only government building restaurant in the world with public access offers gourmet German cuisine and fine views of eastern Berlin.

Platz der Republik 1 feinkost-kaefer.de/berlin

The Reichstag was built between 1884 and 1894 to a Neo-Renaissance design by German architect Paul Wallot. In 1933, a fire destroyed the main hall, and World War II delayed rebuilding for years. In the 1960s, the structure underwent a partial restoration that included the removal of most of the ornamentation on the façade. After German reunification in 1990, the Reichstag once again became the home of the German parliament. The magnificent rooftop glass dome, with its photogenic curves, mirrored columns and stellar views across the city, was added in 1999 by British architect Norman Foster. A permanent exhibition at the dome recalls key events in German parliamentary history.

Did You Know?

A walk taking in the gallery's most famous masterpieces would be 2 km (1 mile) long.

High ceilings and natural light help show off the gallery's masterpieces

GEMÄLDEGALERIE

I6 Matthäikirchplatz 4-6 S & U Potsdamer Platz U Mendelssohn-Bartholdy-Park 200, M29, M41, M48, M85 10am-6pm Tue-Sun (to 8pm Thu) smb.museum

The Picture Gallery is the central attraction of the Kulturforum complex. Circling a striking inner courtyard, the gallery contains many of the world's finest 13th- to 18th-century European paintings.

The paintings in the Picture Gallery collection have been carefully chosen by specialists who, from the beginning of the 19th century, systematically acquired pictures to ensure that all the major European schools of painting were represented. After the division of the city in 1945, the collection was split over several sites in East and West Berlin. Following reunification, with the building of a new home as part of the Kulturforum development, this unique set of paintings was united again. The building was designed by Heinz Hilmer and Christoph Sattler and its exhibition space offers a superb environment in which to view the paintings. The pictures are gently lit by the diffused daylight that streams in from above, while the walls are covered in light-absorbing fabric. The vast hall that occupies the centre of the building allows the visitor to take a break from sightseeing at any time. The hall, with a futuristic sculpture by Walter de Maria set in a water-filled pool, provides an ideal place for moments of quiet contemplation and rest.

The sloped approach to the Kulturforum, obscuring the building within

EAT

Café am Neuen See

For a picturesque, lakeside break between museums, take a stroll to this Tiergarten beer garden.

G6 Lichtensteinallee 2 cafeamneuensee.de

Vox

This elegant hotel restaurant serves a modern fusion of Asian and international dishes.

J6 Marlene-Dietrich-Platz 2 vox-restaurant.de

Lindenbräu

This popular watering hole serves Bavarian specialities and home-brewed fruit-flavoured wheat beer.

J6 Bellevuestrasse 3-5 biergenuss.berlin

POTSDAMER PLATZ

J6 S & U Potsdamer Platz
200, M41, M48, M85, N2
W potsdamerplatz.de

There is no better place to experience the vibrant energy of Berlin than Potsdamer Platz, which has evolved into a thriving city within the city since the fall of the Wall.

Originally a green park in 1831, this square evolved into a major traffic hub thanks to the construction of a railway station, where the city's first ever train made its maiden journey. During the Roaring Twenties, it was Europe's busiest plaza and a bustling entertainment centre, frequented by famous artists and authors. The square was almost destroyed during World War II and was left as a derelict wasteland for decades. Redevelopment began in 1992, and Potsdamer Platz became Europe's largest construction site, where a total of $25 billion has been invested. Now the city's old hub is once again a dynamic centre, with an array of shopping and dining opportunities in modern buildings designed by Renzo Piano, Helmut Jahn and Arata Isozaki.

PICTURE PERFECT
Light Festival

Potsdamer Platz plays a leading role in Berlin's annual Festival of Lights in October. The illuminated installations and light displays are different every year, and are always unforgettable.

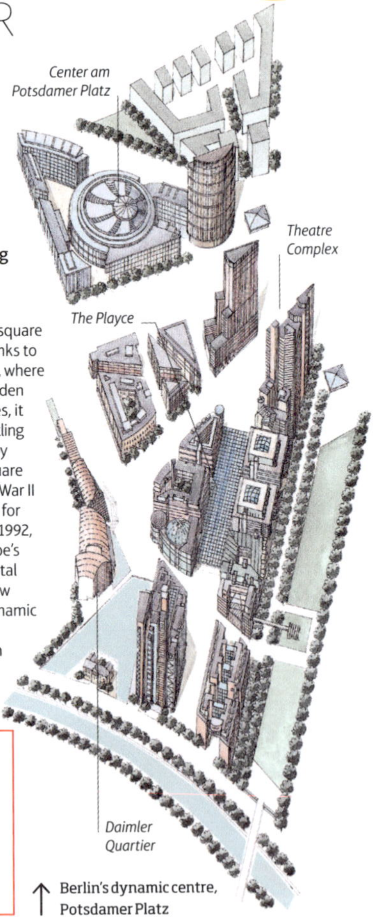

↑ Berlin's dynamic centre, Potsdamer Platz

EXPERIENCE MORE

Philharmonie und Kammermusiksaal

I6 Herbert-von-Karajan-Strasse 1 25 48 88 00 S&U Potsdamer Platz U Mendelssohn-Bartholdy-Park 200, 300, M41, M48, M85

Home to one of the most renowned orchestras in Europe, the Philharmonic and Chamber Music Hall is among the finest post-war architectural achievements in Europe. The Philharmonic, completed in 1963 to a design by Hans Scharoun, pioneered a new concept in concert hall interiors. The orchestra's podium occupies the central section of the penta-gonal hall, around which are galleries for the public, designed to blend into the perspective of the five corners. The exterior reflects the interior and is reminiscent of a circus tent.

The Berlin Philharmonic was founded in 1882 and has been directed by such luminaries as Hans von Bülow, Wilhelm Furtwängler, Sir Simon Rattle and the controversial Herbert von Karajan and Claudio Abbado. The current director is Kirill Petrenko, who took up the position in 2019. The orchestra attained renown not only for the quality of its concerts, but also through its prolific symphony recordings.

The smaller Chamber Music Hall was added in the 1980s. Designed to complement Scharoun's existing architecture, it features a central multisided space covered by a tent-like roof.

Kupferstichkabinett

I6 Matthäikirchplatz 8 S&U Potsdamer Platz U Mendelssohn-Bartholdy-Park 200, M29, M41, M48, M85 10am-6pm daily smb.museum

The print collections of galleries in the former East and West Berlin were united in 1994 in the Print Library, located in the Kulturforum. These displays originated with a collection started by the Great Elector in 1652, which has been open to the public since 1831. Despite wartime losses it has an imposing breadth and features around 2,000 engravers' plates, over 520,000 prints and around 110,000 drawings and watercolours. Sadly, only a small fraction of these delicate treasures can be even briefly exposed to daylight; therefore the museum does not have a permanent exhibition, only galleries with temporary displays of selected works.

The collection includes work from every renowned artist from the Middle Ages to contemporary times. Well represented is the work of Botticelli (including illustrations for Dante's *Divine Comedy*), Dürer, Rembrandt and the Dutch Masters, Watteau, Goya, Daumier and painters of the *Die Brücke* art movement.

↑ The striking home of the Berlin Philharmonic

St-Matthäus-Kirche

I6 Matthäikirchplatz S&U Potsdamer Platz U Mendelssohn-Bartholdy-Park 148, 200, M41, M48, M85 11am-6pm Tue-Sun W stiftung-stmatthaeus.de

St Matthew's Church once stood in the centre of a small square surrounded by buildings. After bomb damage in World War II, the structure was restored, making it the focal point of the Kulturforum. The church was originally constructed between 1844 and 1846, in a style based on Italian Romanesque temples. Each of the three naves is covered by a separate two-tier roof, while the eastern end of the church is closed by a semicircular apse. The exterior is covered in a two-tone brick façade arranged in yellow and red lines. Today, this church with its slender tower, offers an intriguing contrast to the many ultra-modern and sometimes extravagant buildings of the Kulturforum.

Musikinstrumenten-Museum

I6 Tiergartenstrasse 1 S&U Potsdamer Platz 200, M48, M85 Hours vary, check website Mon W sim.spk-berlin.de

Hidden behind the Philharmonie, in a small building designed by Edgar Wisniewski and Hans Scharoun between 1979 and 1984, the fascinating Museum of Musical Instruments houses over 750 exhibits in a collection dating from 1888. Intriguing displays enable you to trace each instrument's development, from the 16th century to the present day. You can marvel at the harpsichord of Jean Marius, once owned by Frederick the Great, and the violins made by Amati and Stradivarius. Most spectacular of all is the silent-film-era cinema organ, a working Wurlitzer dating from 1929. With range of sounds that extends even to locomotive impressions, the demonstrations of its powers every Saturday at noon attract enthusiastic crowds. However, at all times throughout the week the sounds of other exhibited instruments can be heard via recordings. The museum also has an excellent archive and library open to the public, and its calendar of events is full of live concerts.

← Street organ in the Musikinstrumenten-Museum collection

Staatsbibliothek

I7 Potsdamer Strasse 33 S&U Potsdamer Platz 200, M29, M48, M85 9am-9pm Mon-Fri (to 7pm Sat) W staatsbibliothek-berlin.de

An unusually shaped building with an east-facing gilded dome, the State Library is home to one of the largest collections of books and manuscripts in Europe and is fondly referred to by Berliners as the "Stabi". After World War II, East and West

↑ Exhibits at the Schwules Museum, mapping the LGBTQ+ community history

Berlin each inherited part of the prewar state library collection and the Staatsbibliothek was built to house the part belonging to West Berlin. The building itself was designed by Hans Scharoun and Edgar Wisniewski and constructed between 1967 and 1978.

It is a building where the disciplines of function and efficiency take precedence over that of form. The store rooms hold about five million volumes; the hall of the vast reading room is open-plan, with an irregular arrangement of partitions and floor levels; general noise and the sound of footsteps is muffled by fitted carpets, making the interior a very quiet and cosy place in which to work.

The library itself houses more than four million books and an excellent collection of manuscripts. It is formally linked to the Staatsbibliothek on Unter den Linden.

Schwules Museum

H7 Lützowstrasse 73 Nollendorfplatz, Kurfürstenstrasse schwulesmuseum.de

This is the world's first museum dedicated to LGBTQ+ history. Containing more than 50,000 objects, it has four exhibition spaces hosting temporary exhibits, which recount the history and culture of LGBTQ+ communities in Berlin and beyond. Exhibits have included the queer history of video games and LGBTQ+ movements in Germany following Stonewall. The museum also offers film screenings, guided tours and talks on subjects such as celebrity culture and coming out.

Potsdamer Strasse

I7 S&U Potsdamer Platz U Kurfürsten-strasse, Bülowstrasse, Kleistpark 104, 106, 187, 204, M19, M29, M41, M45, M48

A few years ago, Schöneberg's main drag, Potsdamer Strasse, was known for its seedy sex shops and run-down casinos. These days only slight traces of this insalubrious past remain, as gentrification has ushered in a new generation of shops, galleries, cafés and bars. Sitting alongside established spots like the Victoria Bar (No. 102) and the charming Joseph Roth-Diele at No. 75 are shiny new-comers: art galleries such as Circle Culture (No. 75) and Esther Schipper (No. 81e), stylish restaurants such as Irma la Douce (No. 102) and luxury designer shops like Andreas Murkudis (No. 81).

Memorial to Homosexuals Persecuted Under Nazism

J6 Ebertstrasse, Tiergarten

Between 1933 and 1945, tens of thousands of gay men were persecuted, arrested and killed by the Nazis under *Paragraph 175*, a section of Germany's criminal code that made sexual relations between men illegal; around 15,000 were sent to concentration camps. This memorial, established in 2008, is dedicated to their memory, and also acts as a symbol against intolerance and exclusion of the LGBTQ+ community. Designed by Michael Elmgreen and Ingar Dragset, it comprises a single grey concrete cube that is reminiscent of the concrete slabs or "stelae" from the Holocaust Denkmal. A window opens into its interior, where a film is projected; the film alternates biennially, one showing two men kissing and one showing two women kissing.

↑ Contemporary art shown by the nonprofit art collective Urban Nation

Urban Nation

H8 Bülowstrasse 7 U Nollendorfplatz 106, 187, M19 10am-6pm Tue-Sun W urban-nation.com

The Urban Nation Museum For Contemporary Art opened its doors in 2017 in Schöneberg, though its roots as an organization go back to 2013. While the collective behind it, under the curation of Yasha Young, had previously used the city's surfaces as canvasses for outdoor street art and installations, now there is an indoor space to show them off, too. As well as exhibiting the work of international and local artists, the nonprofit venue hosts workshops and events – and it's still possible to find much of their work on the streets around the gallery; look out for the large mural on the corner of Bülow-strasse and Frobenstrasse.

Villa von der Heydt

H7 Von-der-Heydt-Strasse 18 266 41 28 88 U Nollendorfplatz 100, 200, M29

This fine villa, built in a late Neo-Classical style, is one of the few surviving reminders that the southern side of the Tiergarten was one of the most expensive and beautiful residential areas of Berlin. Designed by Hermann Ende and G A Linke, the villa dates from 1862. The neatly manicured gardens and railings around the villa are adorned with busts of Christian Daniel Rauch and Alexander von Humboldt. The statues, by Reinhold Begas, originally lined the Triumphal Avenue in the Tiergarten before being moved here. After restoration in 1980, the villa became the headquarters of one of the most influential cultural bodies, the Foundation of Prussian Cultural Heritage.

Neue Nationalgalerie

I7 Potsdamer Strasse 50 S&U Potsdamer Platz U Mendelssohn-Bartholdy-Park 200, M29, M41, M48, M85 Hours vary, check website smb.museum

The magnificent collection of modern art housed in the New National Gallery has a troubled history. The core of the collection consisted of 262 paintings that belonged to banker J H W Wagener. In the late 1860s, when Wagener died, he left them to Crown Prince William, who housed them in the Nationalgalerie on Museumsinsel.

But, in 1937, a Nazi programme of cultural cleansing meant that over 400 works in the collection, which had grown to include paintings by Monet, Manet and Renoir, were confiscated. After World War II the Berlin municipal authority decided to rebuild the collection and authorized the construction of a suitable building in West Berlin to house it. The commission was given to the elder statesman of modern architecture, the 75-year-old Mies van der Rohe. The result is a striking, minimalist building with a flat steel roof over a glass hall, which appears to float in mid-air supported only by six slender interior struts.

The collection comprises largely 20th-century art, but begins with artists of the late 19th century, such as Edvard Munch, Ferdinand Hodler and Oskar Kokoschka. German movements, such as *Die Brücke*, are well represented, with pieces by Karl Schmidt-Rottluff and Ernst Ludwig Kirchner (notably his evocative oil painting *Potsdamer Platz*).

As well as the Bauhaus movement, represented by Paul Klee and Wassily Kandinsky, the gallery shows works by exponents of a stark realism, such as Otto Dix and George Grosz. Celebrated artists of other European countries are also included – Pablo Picasso, Fernand Léger, de Chirico, Dalí, René Magritte and Max Ernst. Post-World War II art is represented by Barnett Newman, Frank Stella and many others. The sculpture garden houses important works, both figurative and abstract.

Following reunification, new works by artists from the former East Germany were added. Some of the art is sometimes shown at the Hamburger Bahnhof, as both museums draw on the same collection.

DRINK

Potsdamer Strasse has come on leaps and bounds over the last decade, with plenty of great new drinking spots among the cool boutiques and galleries.

Kumpelnest 3000

I7 Lützowstrasse 23 7pm-6am Mon-Thu, 7pm-8am Fri & Sat kumpelnest3000.com

Victoria Bar

I7 Potsdamer Str 102 6:30pm-3am Sun-Thu, 6:30pm-4am Fri & Sat victoriabar.de

Tiger Bar

I7 Potsdamer Strasse 91 6pm-midnight Tue-Sat

Tiergarten

I5 Tiergarten, Bellevue 100, 106, 187, 200, N26

This is the largest park in Berlin. Situated at the geographical centre of the city it occupies a surface area of more than 200 ha (495 acres). Once a forest used as the Elector's hunting reserve, it was transformed into a landscaped park by Peter Joseph Lenné in the 1830s. A Triumphal Avenue was built in the eastern section of the park at the end of the 19th century, lined with statues of the country's rulers and statesmen.

World War II inflicted huge damage on the Tiergarten, including the destruction of the Triumphal Avenue, many of whose surviving monuments can now be seen in the Zitadelle Spandau. Replanting, however, has now restored the Tiergarten, which is a favourite meeting place for Berliners. Its avenues are now lined with statues of figures such as Johann Wolfgang von Goethe and Richard Wagner.

By the lake known as Neuer See and the Landwehrkanal are memorials to the murdered leaders of the Spartacus movement, Karl Liebknecht and Rosa Luxemburg. Also worth finding is a collection of gas lamps, displayed near the Tiergarten S-Bahn station.

Diplomatenviertel

H6 Nollendorfplatz, Potsdamer Platz 100, 106, 187, 200

Although a number of consulates existed in the Tiergarten area as early as 1918, the establishment of a Diplomatic Quarter along the southern edge of the Tiergarten, between Stauffen-bergstrasse and Lichtenstein-allee, did not take place until the period of Hitler's Third Reich, when large embassies representing the Axis Powers, Italy and Japan, were built here.

Despite the fact that these monumental buildings were designed by a number of different architects, the Fascist interpretation of Neo-Classicism and the influence of Albert Speer as head architect meant that the group was homogenous, if bleak. Few buildings survived World War II bombing.

Today, the diplomatic area is bounded by Tiergarten-

strasse. The Austrian embassy, designed by Hans Hollein, stands at the junction of Stauffenbergstrasse, next door to the embassies of India and the Republic of South Africa. At Tiergartenstrasse Nos. 21–3, the pre-World War II Italian embassy still stands, while next door is a copy of the first Japanese embassy. Between Klingelhöferstrasse and Rauchstrasse stands an imposing complex of five embassies. Completed in 1999, these represent Norway, Sweden, Denmark, Finland and Iceland. The complex has an art gallery and café open to the public.

Grosser Stern

G5 Bellevue
Hansaplatz
100, 106, 187, N26

The Great Star roundabout at the centre of the Tiergarten is so-named for the five large roads that radiate from it. At its centre is the enormous Siegessäule (Victory Column). Surrounding it are monuments brought over from the nearby Reichstag building in the late 1930s. During the same period, the Strasse des 17 Juni was widened to twice its original size, the square surrounding the roundabout was enlarged and much of the existing statuary removed.

In the northern section of the square stands a vast bronze monument to the first German Chancellor, Otto von Bismarck (1815–98). Around it stand allegorical figures, the work of late 19th-century sculptor Reinhold Begas. Other statues in the square represent various national heroes including Field Marshal Helmuth von Moltke (1800–91), chief of the Prussian general staff between the years 1858 and 1888, who won the Franco-German war.

SHOP

Andreas Murkudis

One of the first establishments to kick off the ongoing gentrification of this formerly gritty street, this huge, white, bright space stocks a selection of luxury goods curated by the eponymous owner.

I7 Potsdamer Strasse 81 10am-9pm Mon-Sat andreas murkudis.com

← Tiergarten in summer

Haus der Kulturen der Welt

I5 John-Foster-Dulles-Allee 10 S & U Hauptbahnhof, Bundestag 100 10am-7pm daily hkw.de

The House of World Culture, designed by American architect Hugh Stubbins, was intended as the American entry in the international architecture competition "Interbau 1957", from which the Hansaviertel apartment blocks also originated. It soon became a symbol of freedom and modernity in West Berlin during the Cold War, particularly when compared to the GDR-era architecture of Karl-Marx-Allee in East Berlin. Unfortunately its roof failed to withstand the test of time and the building partially collapsed in 1980. After reconstruction it was re-opened in 1989, with a change of purpose: to bring world cultures to a wider German audience via events, exhibitions and performances. It is known for its jazz festivals in particular.

Standing nearby is the black tower of the Carillon, built in 1987 to commemorate the 750th anniversary of Berlin. Suspended in the tower is the largest carillon in Europe, comprising 67 bells. Daily, at noon and 6pm, the bells give a brief computer-controlled concert.

Sowjetisches Ehrenmal

J5 Strasse des 17 Juni S & U Brandenburger Tor 100, 245

The huge Monument to Soviet Soldiers near the Brandenburg Gate was unveiled on 7 November 1945, on the anniversary of the start of the October Revolution in Russia. Flanked by the first two tanks into the city, the monument commemorates over 300,000 Soviet soldiers who perished in the battle for Berlin at the end of World War II. The vast column was made from marble taken from the headquarters of the Chancellor of the Third Reich when it was being dismantled.

The squat structure and parabolic roof of the Haus der Kulturen der Welt

The monument is also a cemetery for around 2,500 Soviet casualties. Following the partition of Berlin, the site ended up in the British sector, but formed a kind of non-territorial enclave to which Soviet soldiers posted to East Berlin had access.

Kunstgewerbe Museum

I6 Matthäikirchplatz 8 S & U Potsdamer Platz U Mendelssohn-Bartholdy-Park 200, M29, M41, M48, M85 10am-6pm Tue-Fri, 11am-6pm Sat & Sun W smb.museum

The Kunstgewerbe Museum embraces many genres of craft and decorative art, from the early Middle Ages to the modern day. Goldwork is especially well represented, and among the most valu able exhibits is an exquisite collection of medieval gold pieces from the church treasuries of Enger, near Herford, and the Guelph treasury from Brunswick. The museum also takes great pride in its collection of late Gothic and Renaissance silver from the town of Lüneburg's civic treasury. There are excellent examples of Italian majolica, and 18th- and 19th-century German, French and Italian glass, porcelain and furniture. Exhibits also include fine pieces of Jugendstil and Art Deco glassware and furniture, and Bauhaus and contemporary design.

Schloss Bellevue

G5 Spreeweg 1 S Bellevue 100, 187

The captivating Bellevue Palace with its dazzlingly white Neo-Classical façade is now the official residence of the German Federal President, and is a very pretty sight from the northern edge of the Tiergarten park. Built in 1786 to a design by Michael Philipp Boumann for the Prussian Prince August Ferdinand, the palace served as a royal residence until 1861. In 1935 it was refurbished to house a Museum of German Ethnology. Refurbished again in 1938, it became a hotel for guests of the Nazi government.

Following bomb damage during World War II, the palace was carefully restored to its former glory, with the oval ballroom rebuilt to a design by Carl Gotthard Langhans. The palace is set within an attractive park laid out to the original late 18th-century design, though unfortunately the picture-sque garden pavilions that once stood here did not survive World War II.

EAT

As well as galleries and cafés, revitalized Potsdamer Strasse has an interesting mix of dining spots.

Irma la Douce

I7 Potsdamer Strasse 102 Mon, Sat L & Sun W irmaladouce.de

Joseph Roth Diele

I7 Potsdamer Strasse 75 10am-midnight Mon-Fri W joseph-roth-diele.de

Facil

J6 Potsdamer Strasse 3 Hours vary, check website W facil.de

€€€

Bendlerblock (Gedenkstätte Deutscher Widerstand)

H6 Stauffenbergstrasse 13-14 26 99 50 00 Potsdamer Platz, Kurfürstenstrasse M29, M48 9am-6pm Mon-Fri (to 8pm Thu), 10am-6pm Sat & Sun

The collection of buildings known as the Bendlerblock was originally built during the Third Reich as an extension to the German State Naval Offices. During World War II these buildings were the headquarters of the Wehrmacht (German Army). It was here that a group of officers planned their famous and ultimately unsuccessful assassination attempt on Hitler on 20 July 1944. Four of the conspirators were shot in the Bendlerblock courtyard, and a monument commemorating this event, designed by Richard Scheibe in 1953, stands where the executions were carried out. On the upper floor of the building is an exhibition documenting the history of the German anti-Nazi movements.

Regierungsviertel

I4 Brandenburger Tor Bundestag 100, 248

This bold concept for a government district fit for a 21st-century capital was the winning design in a competition held in 1992. Construction of the complex was completed in 2003. Axel Schultes and Charlotte Frank's grand design proposed a rectangular site cutting across the meander of the Spree just north of the Reichstag.

While many of the buildings have been designed by other architects to fit within the overall concept, Schultes and Frank designed the Bundeskanzleramt, opposite the Reichstag – the official residence of the German Chancellor. The whole project is complemented by the neighbouring Hauptbahnhof railway station, an impressive glass-and-steel construction with several levels above and below ground. The U-Bahn line U5 has been extended and now connects Hauptbahnhof with the Brandenburg Gate, Unter den Linden, Museum Island and Alexanderplatz.

Siegessäule

G5 Grosser Stern 391 29 61 Bellevue Hansaplatz 100, 106, 187 Apr-Oct: 9:30am-6:30pm daily; Nov-Mar: 10am-5pm daily

The Victory Column is based on a design by Johann Heinrich Strack and was built to commemorate Prussia's triumph in the Prusso-Danish war of 1864.

After further Prussian victories, "Goldelse", a gilded figure by Friedrich Drake representing Victory, was added to the top. The monument stood in front of the Reichstag building until the Nazi government moved it here in 1938. The base is

←
The Regierungsviertel's Marie-Elisabeth-Lüders-Haus office building (2003), named for one of Germany's first female politicians

decorated with bas-reliefs commemorating battles. Higher up the column, a mosaic frieze depicts the 1871 founding of the German Empire. An observation terrace at the top offers magnificent vistas over Berlin.

Bauhaus-Archiv

H7 Klingelhöferstrasse 14 25 40 02 78 Nollendorfplatz 100, 106, 187, M29 For restoration

The Bauhaus school of art, started by Walter Gropius in 1919, was one of the most influential art institutions of the 20th century. The belief of the Bauhaus group was that art and technology should combine in harmonious unity.

Originally based in Weimar, and from 1925 in Dessau, this school provided inspiration for numerous artists and architects. Staff and students included Mies van der Rohe, Paul Klee, Wassily Kandinsky, Theo van Doesburg and László Moholy-Nagy. The school moved to Berlin in 1932, but was closed down by the Nazis in 1933.

After the war, the Bauhaus-Archiv was relocated to Darmstadt. In 1964 Walter Gropius designed a building to house the collection, but it was never realized. The archive was moved to Berlin in 1971, where the design was adapted to the new site. The gleaming white building with its distinctive glass-panelled gables was completed in 1979, and while the interior is closed for renovation, the exterior is magnificent. Some of the archive (together with its Bauhaus shop) can be seen in its temporary home in the Hardenberg Haus, on the corner of Knesebeckstrasse and Hardenbergstrasse, not far from Berlin Zoo.

Hansaviertel

G4 Bellevue Hansaplatz 100, 106, 187

This area to the west of Schloss Bellevue is home to some of the most interesting modern architecture in Berlin, built for an international exhibition in 1957. Taking on a World War II bomb site, prominent architects from around the world designed 45 projects, of which 36 were realized, to create a varied residential development set in an environment of lush greenery. The list of distinguished architects involved in the project included Walter Gropius (Händelallee Nos. 3–9), Alvar Aalto (Klopstockstrasse Nos. 30–32) and Oscar Niemeyer (Altonaer Strasse Nos. 4–14). The development also includes a school, a commercial services building and two churches.

In 1960, a new headquarters for the Akademie der Künste (Academy of Arts) was built at Hanseatenweg No. 10. Designed by Werner Düttmann, the academy has a concert hall, an exhibition area, archives and a library. In front of the main entrance is a magnificent piece, *Reclining Figure*, by eminent British sculptor Henry Moore.

KREUZBERG

One of Berlin's most dynamic districts, Kreuzberg can be divided into several unofficial "zones". The northern section can be considered part of the tourist centre, with several significant sights and museums. The eastern section, sometimes referred to as SO36, is decidedly alternative, with a buzzy nightlife and a large concentration of Turkish and Middle Eastern immigrants. In contrast, Western Kreuzberg is more gentrified, characterised by pleasant cafés, tree-lined avenues and the historical Viktoriapark.

↓ Café patrons enjoying a summer evening in Kreuzberg

Iron plate faces *(inset)* lie discarded on the floor in Menashe Kadishman's *Shalekhet* installation

JÜDISCHES MUSEUM BERLIN

L7 Lindenstrasse 9-14 Hallesches Tor, Kochstrasse M29, M41, 248 10am-7pm daily Some Jewish hols jmberlin.de

The Jewish Museum is a mix of exhibition spaces, archives and gardens that bring the memories and stories of Jewish culture alive.

MUSEUM GUIDE

Entrance to the main museum (the Libeskind Building) is via an underground tunnel. The exhibition is divided into 14 sections, taking visitors through German Jewish history and culture from early history up to the present day.

Designed by Daniel Libeskind, a Polish-Jewish architect based in the United States, the museum complex is an exciting and imaginative example of late 20th-century architecture. The complex contains a library and gardens, but the highlight of the museum is the Libeskind Building, whose shape, style and interior arrangement are part of a philosophical programme to illustrate the history and culture of Germany's Jewish community, and the repercussions of the Holocaust. The long, narrow galleries with slanting floors and sharp zigzagging turns are designed to evoke the feeling of loss and dislocation. These are interspersed by "voids" that represent the vacuum left behind by the destruction of Jewish life.

↑ Swiss Air Force Bü 131 biplane in the superb Aerospace exhibition

EAT

Tomasa

This red-brick villa has a well-stocked playroom, a great kids' menu and a courtyard and garden. It's a good spot for breakfast before the museum.

J10 Kreuzbergstrasse 62 9am-midnight Sun-Wed, 9am-1am Thu tomasa.de

DEUTSCHES TECHNIKMUSEUM BERLIN

J8 Trebbiner Strasse 9 Gleisdreieck M29, M41 9am-5:30pm Tue-Fri, 10am-6pm Sat & Sun technikmuseum.berlin

The Museum of Technology takes visitors on a multimedia journey through recent human history by exploring its technological achievements.

The museum was established by grouping together more than 100 smaller, specialized collections under one roof. The current collection is arranged on the site of a former trade hall, the size of which allows many of the museum's exhibits – such as locomotives, aircraft, boats and water towers – to be displayed full-size and in their original condition. Highlights of the collec-tion include vintage cars and motorcycles, and dozens of locomotives and railway carriages from different eras. There are also exhibitions dedicated to flying, printing, weaving, engineering and computer technology. Live demonstrations of machinery are held regularly; the schedule is available at the information desk in the entrance hall. Next to the museum is a park containing two windmills and the museum's rail transport exhibit in the former Anhalter Bahnhof station.

EXPERIENCE MORE

Martin-Gropius-Bau

K7 Niederkirchner Strasse 7 (corner of Stresemannstrasse) 25 48 60 S & U Potsdamer Platz 200, M29, M41 10am-7pm Wed-Mon

The innovative Martin-Gropius-Bau building was originally built to fulfil the requirements of an arts and crafts museum. It was designed by Martin Gropius with the participation of Heino Schmieden and constructed in 1881. The building's style is reminiscent of an Italian Renaissance palace, with a magnificent glazed interior courtyard, an impressive atrium and unusual, richly decorated elevations. Located between the windows are the crests of German cities, and within the friezes are reliefs illustrating different arts and crafts. In the plaques between the windows of the top storey are beautiful mosaics containing allegorical figures representing the cultures of different eras and countries. From 1922, Martin-Gropius-Bau accommodated the Museum of Ethnology, but after World War II the building was abandoned and left in ruins. Although plans for an inner-city motorway threatened it until the 1970s, a reconstruction programme eventually commenced in 1981, led by architects Winnetou Kampmann and Ute Weström.

This was followed in 1999 by a further refurbishment, and since then the building has housed a changing series of exhibitions on art, photography and architecture.

Science Center Spectrum

J8 Möckernstrasse 26 S Anhalter Bahnhof U Möckernbrücke, Gleisdreieck M29, M41, 248 Hours vary, check website W sdtb.de/spectrum

This annexe to the Deutsches Technikmuseum focuses on interactive exhibits. With its own distinct building next to the main museum, it occupies some 1,400 sq m (15,000 sq ft) of space across four floors, and features around 150 interactive exhibits arranged by themes such as Sound, Light & Sight and Power. There's a big room full of cars and motorbikes, a rainbow suspended in the air without the use of water, and masses of hands-on experiments, including swings and bridges to operate, the option to create colour tones by mixing light surfaces originating from real sunlight, and a Foucault's Pendulum that shows how the earth rotates. Last but not least there's a fun hall of mirrors for some stretchy selfies.

Berlin Story Bunker

J7 Schöneberger Strasse 23A S Anhalter Bahnhof U Mendelssohn-Bartholdy-Park M29, M41 10am-7pm daily W berlinstory.de

The bunker that houses this idiosyncratic museum was used during the war by those working in and living around the nearby Anhalter Bahnhof train station, which is now a memorial ruin. Today it contains the Berlin Story Museum, which illuminates some of the most significant aspects of Berlin's 800-year history through multimedia stations that combine photographs, films and art installations.

A separate exhibition was added in 2017 entitled "Hitler – how could it happen." It follows the timeline of Adolf Hitler's rise and fall via photographs, films, documents and recreations of parts of the infamous Führerbunker.

Sommerbad Kreuzberg

M8 Prinzenstrasse 113-9 30 22 19 00 11 Prinzenstrasse 140, 248 7am-8pm daily

Known more commonly as Prinzenbad due to its proximity to the Prinzenstrasse U-Bahn station, this cult Kreuzberg swimming pool was made famous by its appearance in Sven Regener's 2001 book *Herr Lehmann* – and it subsequently featured in the hit film, too. While not the most refined of the city's pools, its two 50-m (164-ft) pools are hugely popular not only for their outdoor location, but also because they're big on character. Expect to find a rich and varied mix of hipsters, Middle Eastern families, elderly Berliners and water-sliding youngsters gathered here on any warm day.

Mehringplatz

L8 Hallesches Tor 248, M41

Mehringplatz was planned in the 1730s when the boundaries of the city were extended. Its original name was Rondell, meaning "circus", an appropriate name, as Wilhelmstrasse, Friedrichstrasse and Lindenstrasse all converged here. Rondell was originally the work of Philipp Gerlach; then, in the 1840s, Peter Joseph Lenné designed the decoration of the square. At the centre is the Column of Peace, commemorating the Wars of Liberation in 1815. The column is crowned by the figure of Victory by Christian Daniel Rauch. Two sculptures were added in the 1870s: *Peace* by Albert Wolff and *Clio* (the Muse of History) by Ferdinand Hartzer. In the 19th and early 20th centuries the area was populated with politicians, diplomats and aristocrats, and in 1947 the square was named after the writer Franz Mehring. The current buildings date from the 1970s.

Kottbusser Tor

N8 Kottbusser Strasse Kottbusser Tor 140, M29, N8

Nicknamed "Little Istanbul", Kottbusser Tor has long been the Turkish heartland of inner city Berlin. Originally a city gate leading to the city of Cottbus, today it's ostensibly a roundabout surrounded by 1970s- and 1980s era residential housing bedecked with tell-tale satellite dishes (so that residents can tune into Turkish and Middle Eastern TV channels). It's a vibrant area whether day or night, with a constant flow of foot and car traffic and a procession of food markets, street vendors and coffee shops. Although its reputation for low-level crime can't be disregarded, these days it's mostly frequented by a mix of local families and hipsters who congregate at weekends in search of the many inconspicuous bars and clubs – Monarch, Palermo, Möbel Olfe – as well as the mix of cheap falafel spots and trendy US-style burger joints like The Bird.

FHXB Museum

O8 Adalbertstrasse 95A Kottbusser Tor 140, M29 Noon-8pm Tue-Thu, 10am-8pm Fri-Sun fhfhxb-museum.de

Housed in an old furniture factory away from the hustle and bustle of nearby Kottbusser Tor, the FHXB Museum, named after Berlin's Friedrichshain-Kreuzberg borough, charts the tumultuous and, at times, radical past of this vibrant neighbourhood. Permanent exhibitions at this community museum explore how 40 years of urban regeneration policies have defined the area, and the protest movements against its gentrification. An

↑ Outside alternative music venue SO36, known for its techno and indie sounds

interactive exhibit enables visitors to listen to locals' stories, and they can walk over a large map of Kreuzberg, discovering various places in the district from the perspective of residents and refugee new Berliners. A lively roster of talks and workshops covers themes such as immigration and the housing crisis, which are top of mind to residents.

SO36

O8 Oranienstrasse 190 Kottbusser Tor M29, 140 9pm-5am Tue-Sat so36.de

One of Berlin's best-known alternative music venues, SO36 – the name is a reference to the district's Berlin Wall-era postal code – grew famous during the 1970s and 1980s, when it was run by artist Martin Kippenberger and hosted edgy punk and post-punk acts like Iggy Pop, Nick Cave and Einstürzende Neubauten. Today it regularly hosts big-name bands, mostly of a rock and indie persuasion, as well as up-and-coming local bands in its basic, large main room. Look out also for regular specials such as roller discos, Turkish LGBTQ+ pop event Gayhane and even the occasional flea market.

Hansa Studios

J7 Köthener Strasse 38 For tours only; book via the website musictoursberlin.de

Hansa Studios is one of Berlin's most famous music recording studios. Built in 1912, it has recorded albums by such internationally renowned names as David Bowie, Depeche Mode, U2 and R.E.M., as well as German luminaries such as Nina Hagen and Udo Jürgens. Only one studio is active these days, but it's possible to tour the building and also see the rooms where many of these prominent artists once recorded.

SHOP

Voo Store

Situated inside a former locksmith's shop, this swanky industrial-design studio sells a highly curated mix of clothing, home decor and fashion accessories. Great coffee shop, too.

O8
Oranienstrasse 24
11am-7pm Mon-Sat
vooberlin.com

Stark white interiors of the modern Berlinische Galerie

Berlinische Galerie

L7 Alte Jakobstrasse 124-8 Kochstrasse 248, M29 10am-6pm Wed-Mon berlinische galerie.de

The city's museum for modern art, design and architecture is one of the finest regional museums in the country. Changing themed exhibitions draw upon its huge collection of German, East European and Russian paintings, photographs, graphics and architectural artifacts.

One of the highlights is the 5,000-strong painting collection, which covers all the major art movements from the late 19th century until today. It includes works by Max Liebermann, Otto Dix, Georg Baselitz, Alexander Rodchenko, Iwan Puni and Via Lewandowsky.

The museum's collection of sketches, prints and posters encompasses the Berlin Dadaists George Grosz, Hannah Höch and Werner Heldt, as well as works by Ernst Ludwig Kirchner and Hanns Schimansky.

Among the architectural items held by the Galerie are drawings and models for buildings that were never built, offering fascinating glimpses into how the city might have looked. A fine example is the shell-like Expressionist Sternkirche (Star Church), designed by Otto Bartning in 1922.

Topographie des Terrors

K7 Stresemann-strasse 110 (entrance on Niederkirchner Strasse 8) S & U Potsdamer Platz, Kochstrasse S Anhalter Bahnhof M29, M41 10am-8pm daily topographie.de

During the Third Reich, three of the most terrifying Nazi political departments had their headquarters in a block here, making this area the government district of National Socialist Germany. Prinz-Albrecht palace at Wilhelmstrasse No. 102 became the headquarters of the Third Reich's security service (SD). Prinz-Albrecht-Strasse No. 8 was occupied by the head of the Gestapo, Heinrich Müller, while the Hotel Prinz Albrecht at No. 9 became the headquarters of Himmler's SS.

After World War II, the ruins of the heavily bombed buildings were pulled down. In 1987, however, an exhibition was installed on this site by committed citizens of Berlin. This well-researched and exhaustive exploration of Nazi crimes and terror in all its forms, including propaganda, deportation, forced labour and genocide, builds a chilling picture of the decisions that must have been taken on this very site. A preserved section of the Berlin Wall runs alongside the building, on Niederkirchner Strasse.

König Gallery (St Agnes)

M8 Alexandrinen-strasse 118-121 U Prinzenstrasse, Moritzplatz 140, 248, N41 11am-7pm Tue-Sat, noon-7pm Sun koeniggalerie.com

The striking, almost windowless Brutalist church

of St Agnes was built in the 1960s. It houses the Johann König Gallery, which opened here in 2015 following a renovation by Arno Brandlhuber. The gallery features two distinctive spaces – one on the main floor and one on an upper floor supported by a concrete slab – plus a sculpture garden that also forms part of the exhibitions. In addition to solo shows and group exhibitions, the gallery hosts regular readings, performances and presentations. There's a pleasant café inside too, and some of the surrounding buildings are used by artists during their residencies.

Checkpoint Charlie

L6 Friedrichstrasse 43-45 Kochstrasse M29

Between 1961 and 1990, Checkpoint Charlie was the only crossing point for foreigners between East and West Berlin. During that time, it represented a symbol of both freedom and separation for the many East Germans trying to escape from the GDR regime. It was also witness to dramatic events during the Cold War, including a tense two-day standoff between Russian and American tanks in 1961. Little remains of the checkpoint: no gates, barriers or barbed wire. Instead, there is a replica checkpoint booth and the famous huge sign on the old Western side that reads "You are leaving the American Sector".

At the museum nearby, Haus am Checkpoint Charlie, look out for the exhibits connected with the escape attempts of East Germans to the West. The ingenuity and bravery of these escapees are astonishing, using devices such as secret compartments built into cars and specially constructed suitcases.

Moritzplatz

N7 Moritzplatz 140, M29

For several decades – before and after the fall of the Wall – the area around Moritzplatz was a somewhat bleak vision of 1970s residential blocks and the occasional kebab shop. Since then, it has been transformed almost beyond recognition by a flurry of developments. It has been joined by the creative centre Aufbau Haus, which houses the Aufbau publishing group, a bookshop, arts and design shops, a crafts supplier called Modular, a CLB-Berlin project space for contemporary art and urbanism, and the Kai Dikhas contemporary Sinti and Roma art gallery.

EAT & DRINK

Cocolo

The second branch of Berlin's best ramen spot. Cocolo's menu is small but consistently top-notch: think ramen with sweet pork belly or miso and vegetables, plus extras like Japanese dumplings.

O8 Paul-Lincke-Ufer 39 Noon-11pm Mon-Sat kuchi.de/restaurant/cocolo-x-berg

Luzia

One of the district's most popular pre-club bars. A welcoming and quirky mix of exposed brick walls, street art murals and floor-to-ceiling windows that are ideal for people-watching.

O7 Oranienstrasse 34 30 81 79 99 58 Noon-5am daily

GREAT VIEW
Top of the World

Berlin's highest natural peak can be found at the top of Kreuzberg's Viktoriapark, alongside a tumbling waterfall, a war memorial by Karl Friedrich Schinkel and stellar views towards the city centre.

Viktoriapark

K10 Platz der Luftbrücke 104, 140, M19

This rambling park, with several artificial waterfalls, short trails and a small hill, was designed by Hermann Mächtig and built between 1884 and 1894. The Neo-Gothic Memorial to the Wars of Liberation at the summit of the hill is the work of Karl Friedrich Schinkel, which commemorates the Prussian victory against Napoleon's army in the Wars of Liberation. The cast-iron tower is well ornamented. In the niches of the lower section are 12 allegorical figures by Christian Daniel Rauch, Friedrich Tieck and Ludwig Wichmann. Each figure symbolizes a battle and is linked to a historic figure – either a military leader or a member of the royal family. The park contains the popular Golgotha pub and beer garden, perfect for refreshment after a stroll.

← Viktoriapark's Neo-Gothic memorial

Flughafen Tempelhof and Tempelhofer Feld

K10 Platz der Luftbrücke 200 03 74 41 Platz der Luftbrücke 104, 248

The disused Tempelhof Airport was once Germany's biggest. Built in 1923, it was enlarged during the Third Reich. You can take a guided tour of the building (1:30pm on Wed, Fri, Sat and Sun), which is typical of Third Reich architecture, even though the eagles that decorate it predate the Nazis. In 1951, a monument was added in front of the airport. Designed by Eduard Ludwig, it commemorates the airlifts of the Berlin Blockade.The three spikes on the top symbolize the air corridors used by Allied planes.

The airport was permanently closed to air traffic in 2008. It has now been transformed into a park that is popular with cyclists, roller-bladers and skaters who come here to enjoy the unobstructed airport runways.

Riehmers Hofgarten

K9 Yorckstrasse 83-86, Grossbeerenstrasse 56-57 & Hagelberger Strasse 9-12 Mehringdamm 140, 248, M19

Riehmers Hofgarten is the name given to the 20 or so exquisite houses arranged around a picturesque garden within the area bordered by the streets Yorckstrasse, Hagelberger Strasse and Grossbeerenstrasse. These houses were built between 1881 and 1899 to the detailed designs of Wilhelm Riehmer and Otto Mrosk, respected architects who not only designed the houses' intricate, Renaissance-style and Neo-Baroque façades but also gave equal splendour to the elevations overlooking the courtyard garden. The streets of Riehmers Hofgarten have been carefully restored and Yorckstrasse also has quite a few cafés.

Next to Riehmers Hofgarten is the church of St Bonifaz, designed by Max Hasak. Adjacent to the church is a similar complex of houses built in an impressive Neo-Gothic style.

Outdoor dining in summer on busy Bergmannstrasse

Bergmannstrasse

K9 Südstern, Geneisenaustrasse 248, N7, N6, N42

Kreuzberg is unofficially divided between its gritty and hip east side and its more gentrified western counterpart. Here, entire blocks of 19th-century houses have been restored and the area's main artery, Bergmannstrasse, has been revitalized. Pedestrianized and furnished with antique streetlamps to enhance the atmosphere, it bristles with independent shops, galleries, cafés and restaurants. Also refreshed is the popular Marheineke Markthalle: a covered market filled with not only fruit and vegetables but also cafés, delis and even exhibitions. Just off the street is the charming Chamissoplatz, which draws crowds to its Saturday morning organic farmers' market. To the west, the street leads to one of the main parks in the area, Viktoriapark, ideal for a green breather after the bustle of the streets.

Anhalter Bahnhof

K7 Askanischer Platz 6-7 Anhalter Bahnhof Potsdamer Platz, Mendelssohn-Bartholdy-Park M29, M41

Only a tiny fragment now remains of the Anhalter Bahnhof station, which was named after the Saxon royal family. It was once Berlin's largest, and Europe's second-largest, railway station. The hugely ambitious structure was designed by Franz Schwechten and constructed in 1880. The station was intended to be the biggest and most elegant in Europe in order to impress official visitors to the capital of the German Empire. Some of the most famous people to alight at Anhalter Bahnhof were the Italian King Umberto, who was welcomed by Kaiser Wilhelm II himself, and the Russian Tsar Nicholas.

The station was taken out of public use in 1943 after its roof was completely destroyed by Allied bombing. Only the front portico remains, crowned by still-damaged sculptures and the hole that housed a large electric clock, as well as fragments of its once glorious façade. On the vast grounds behind rises the soaring, tent-like roof of the entertainment venue, Tempodrom.

Friedhöfe vor dem Halleschen Tor

L9 Mehringdamm, Blücher, Baruther & Zossener Strasse 691 61 38 Hallesches Tor 140, 248, M41 Hours vary, call ahead

Beyond the city walls, next to the Hallesches Gate, are four cemeteries established in 1735. The beautiful gravestones commemorate some of Berlin's greatest artists, including writer, painter and composer E T A Hoffmann, composer Felix Mendelssohn-Bartholdy, and architects Carl Ferdinand Langhans, Georg Wenzeslaus von Knobelsdorff and David Gilly.

AROUND KURFÜRSTENDAMM

Kurfürstendamm – usually abbreviated to the more manageable "Ku'damm" – is a 3.5-km- (2.2-mile-) long boulevard beginning at bustling Breitscheidplatz, close to the historical Zoological Garden and the distinctive Kaiser Wilhelm Memorial Church. It's lined on both sides with a non-stop mix of upscale fashion boutiques and high-street stores, and punctuated throughout with cafés, restaurants, hotels and cultural venues. Its side streets are also well worth exploring.

↓ KaDeWe seen from Bahnhof Wittenbergplatz U-bahn station

Must See

KAISER WILHELM GEDÄCHTNIS KIRCHE

F7 Breitscheidplatz S&U Zoologischer Garten U Kurfürstendamm 100, 109, 110, 200, 204, 245, M19, M29, M46, X10, X34 9am-7pm daily gedaechtniskirche-berlin.de

The damaged tower of Kaiser Wilhelm Memorial Church is a symbol of peace and the city's determination to rebuild after World War II.

This church-monument is one of Berlin's most famous landmarks, surrounded by a lively crowd of street traders, buskers and beggars. The vast Neo-Romanesque church was designed by Franz Schwechten and consecrated in 1895. It was almost completely destroyed by Allied bombs in 1943, and after World War II the ruins were removed, leaving only the massive front tower at the base of which the *Gedenkhalle* (Memorial Hall) is situated. This hall documents the history of the church and contains some of its original ceiling mosaics, marble reliefs and liturgical objects. In 1961, Egon Eiermann designed an octagonal church in blue glass and a new freestanding bell tower.

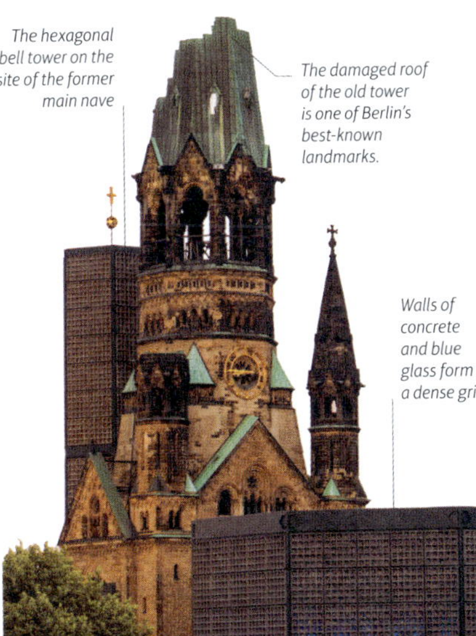

The hexagonal bell tower on the site of the former main nave

The damaged roof of the old tower is one of Berlin's best-known landmarks.

Walls of concrete and blue glass form a dense grid

COVENTRY AND BERLIN

In the main entrance of the old church you'll find a surprisingly modest crucifix. It was fashioned from nails found in the ashes of Coventry Cathedral, England, which was destroyed during German bombing raids in 1940.

The old spire, completed in 1895, and the new church and bell tower, completed in 1961

EXPERIENCE MORE

KaDeWe

F7 Tauentzienstrasse 21-4 U Wittenbergplatz M19, M29, M46 10am-8pm Mon-Thu, 10am-9pm Fri, 9:30am-8pm Sat kadewe.de

Kaufhaus des Westens, or KaDeWe, is the largest department store in Europe. It was built in 1907 to a design by Emil Schaudt, but it has been extended several times. From the very beginning it was Berlin's most exclusive department store, with a slogan that ran "In our shop a customer is a king, and the king is a customer". After World War II, KaDeWe became the symbol of the economic success of West Berlin.

You can buy everything here; however, the main attraction must be the Food Hall, a gourmet's paradise, with luscious fruits and vegetables, live fish and seafood, 100 varieties of tea, more than 2,400 wines and a host of other gastronomic delights. KaDeWe also has a restaurant, the Wintergarten.

Bikinihaus Mall

F7 Budapester Strasse 38-50 S & U Zoologischer Garten U Kurfürstendamm 100, 110, 200, 204, 245, 249, M45 10am-8pm Mon-Sat bikiniberlin.de

The three-floor Bikinihaus Mall, named for the 1950s building that houses it, has an inspired feature: its ground floor houses 70 wooden "pop-ups", crate-like mini-shops that independent stores can rent for up to a year. This keeps things fresh and exciting while the surrounding brand outlets, such as Carhaart, Scotch & Soda, Gant, offer a solid range of mid-range fashion and home design.

Europa-Center

F7 Breitscheidplatz S & U Zoologischer Garten 100, 109, 200

The Europa-Center stands on the site of the legendary Romanisches Café, a famous meeting place for Dada artists in the 1920s. The current building dates from 1965, and since that time it has been one of the largest complexes of its type in the whole of Germany. Designed by Helmut Hentrich and Hubert Petschnigg, it comprises a group of low-rise buildings housing a trade centre, numerous restaurants and pubs, the

Food with a view at legendary department store KaDeWe

GREAT VIEW
Monkey Bar

As well as amazing cocktails, the Monkey Bar at the 25hours Hotel Bikini has a wrap-around terrace with excellent views over the adjacent zoo and Kaiser Wilhelm Gedächtnis Kirche.

deluxe Hotel Palace Berlin and the political cabaret *Die Stachelschweine*.

Around the Center are some intriguing fountains, including the "Flow of Time Clock", designed by Bernard Gitton. Seconds, minutes and hours are measured in vials and spheres of green liquid.

Newton-Sammlung and Museum für Fotografie

E6 Jebensstrasse 2 S & U Zoologischer Garten 10am-6pm Tue, Wed & Fri-Sun; 9am-8pm Thu W smb.museum

Society and art photographer Helmut Newton (1931–2004) bequeathed his life's work to the city of Berlin. Newton, who was born and received his first training as a photographer in Berlin, became one of the 20th century's most well-known photographers with his stark black-and-white images of nudes and portraits of the rich and famous. This museum serves as the city's museum of photography, and is constantly expanding its collections. It displays photographs dating back to the 19th century, and its exhibits on Newton contain selections of his work – including fashion and landscapes – as well as a collection of his cameras.

Zoo Berlin

F7 Hardenbergplatz 8/Budapester Strasse 34 S & U Zoologischer Garten 100, 109, 110, 200, 204, 245, 249, M45, M46, M49, X10, X34 Hours vary, check website W zoo-berlin.de

Zoo Berlin is one of Berlin's most popular attractions and over 1,000 species are to be found here. Part of the Tiergarten, it dates from 1844, which makes it the oldest zoo in Germany. You can enter from Hardenbergplatz through the Lion's Gate, and from Budapester Strasse through the decorative Elephant Gate. The zoo offers a number of attractions, including the monkey house, with its family of gorillas, and a darkened pavilion for nocturnal animals. The hippopotamus pool has a glazed wall so they can be seen underwater. Since 2017, the zoo has also been home to a pair of giant pandas. The aquarium, one of the largest in Europe, contains sharks, piranhas and unusual animals from coral reefs. There is also a huge terrarium with an overgrown jungle that is home to a group of crocodiles.

Tauentzienstrasse

F7 U Wittenbergplatz M19, M29, M46

This is one of the most important streets for trade and commerce in this part of Berlin. Some shops here are not as expensive or as elegant as on Kurfürstendamm – but they attract more visitors for this reason. One of the highlights of the street is the unusual façade of the department store Peek & Cloppenburg. Designed by Gottfried Böhm, the walls of the building are covered with transparent, gently slanting and undulating "aprons". Also unmissable, literally, is the amazing sculpture, *Berlin*. Representing the divided Berlin of the Wall era, it was installed in 1987 to mark the 750th anniversary of the city.

Savignyplatz

D7 Savignyplatz M49, X34

Savignyplatz is enclosed on the south side by the arcade of a railway viaduct, under which Sally (Liza Minnelli) and Brian (Michael York) scream in the film *Cabaret* by Bob Fosse. During the day the square does not look interesting – there are no remarkable buildings, only carefully tended greenery and flowerbeds. However, the area around the square truly comes alive at night, when the dozens of cafés and restaurants fill up. During summer, the entire edge of Savignyplatz and neighbouring streets turn into one big garden filled with tables and umbrellas. People come from outlying districts to visit popular restaurants and cafés such as Dicke Wirtin. The arcades in the viaduct contain many cafés and bars, and one section has been taken up by the Bücherbogen bookshop.

Theater des Westens

E7 Kantstrasse 9-12 0180 544 44 S & U Zoologischer Garten 100, 109, 110, 200, M49, X10, X34

The Theater of the West, one of the most picturesque of all Berlin's theatres, was built in 1896 to a design by Bernhard Sehring. The composition of its façade links Neo-Classical elements with Palladian and Art Nouveau details. The interior of the theatre has been designed in a splendid Neo-Baroque style, while the back and the section that houses the stage have been rebuilt within a Neo-Gothic structure, incorporating the decorative elements of a chess set.

From its very beginning the theatre focused on lighter forms of musical entertainment. Operettas and vaudeville have been staged here, and in more recent times musicals such as *Les Misérables*. Some of the world's greatest stars have appeared on the stage here, including Josephine Baker, who performed her famous banana dance in 1926. Near the theatre is the renowned Delphi cinema and popular jazz club Quasimodo.

C/O Berlin

E7 Hardenbergstrasse 22-4 U Zoologischer Garten 100, 200, 245, M49, X10, X34 11am-8pm daily co-berlin.org

This photography exhibition centre showcases work by renowned photographers as well as young talent, and holds artist talks, lectures and guided tours. It is housed in Amerika Haus, the former American culture and information centre, built during the international building exhibition in 1956–7 to a light and airy design by Bruno Grimmek.

Fasanenstrasse

E7 U Uhlandstrasse 109, 110, M49, X10, X34

The discreet charm of Fasanenstrasse, particularly between Lietzenburger Strasse and Kurfürstendamm,

has attracted the most exclusive designer shops in the world. *Fin-de-siècle* villas set in tranquil gardens and elegant shop windows of jewellers, art galleries and fashion shops will all entice you to take an afternoon stroll along this street.

It is worth seeing the villas at No. 23–25, which are called the Wintergarten-Ensemble – No. 23 dates from 1889. Tucked away in a garden, the villa is home to the Literaturhaus, which organizes interesting exhibitions and readings (closed for renovation until 2027). It also houses a café that extends into a conservatory. No. 25, built in 1892 by Hans Grisebach, has an auction house and art gallery.

Steinplatz

E6 Steinplatz S & U Ernst-Reuter-Platz, Zoologischer Garten 245, M45, N2

Because of the two nearby universities (Berlin University of the Arts and the Technical University of Berlin), this square was a popular meeting place for artists, intellectuals and students in the years of West Berlin. A green oasis surrounded by beautiful architecture, the square is still a lovely meeting spot, and makes a great place to take a break while exploring the galleries and stores along Hardenbergstrasse, and in the streets between here and Savignyplatz.

The square also contains a monument dedicated to the victims of Stalinism and National Socialism. It is made of stones from Fasanenstrasse Synagogue, which was destroyed during World War II.

Crowds outside the C/O Berlin photography exhibit centre

Jüdisches Gemeindehaus

E7 Fasanenstrasse 79/80 88 02 80 S & U Zoologischer Garten U Uhlandstrasse or Kurfürstendamm 245, M49, X10, X34

The Jewish Community House is the headquarters of the local Jewish community, constructed on the site of a synagogue that was burned down by the Nazis and their supporters during Kristallnacht on 9 November 1938. The new building, designed by Dieter Knoblauch and Heinz Heise, was constructed in 1959. The only reminders of the splendour of the former synagogue are the portal at the entrance to the building and some decorative fragments on the façade. Inside there are offices and a prayer room covered by three glazed domes. At the rear there is a courtyard with a place of remembrance. There is also an emotive statue at the front of the building, depicting a broken scroll of the Torah (the holy book of Jewish law).

EAT & DRINK

Lon Men's Noodle House

Family-run Taiwanese that's small in size but big on taste. Try the dumplings or ask for the homemade noodles.

D7 Kantstrasse 33 030 31 51 96 78 Noon–10:30pm daily

Bar am Steinplatz

This famous and stylish hotel bar was a meeting place for artists in West Berlin in the 1960s. Since its rebirth in 2014 it is again attracting up-market bar-hoppers.

D7 Steinplatz 4 barsteinplatz.com

AROUND SCHLOSS CHARLOTTENBURG

One of Berlin's premier royal sights, the Schloss Charlottenburg palace complex is almost a small village in itself. Its ensemble of extravagant Baroque buildings include former royal apartments, rooms brimming with antique porcelain and prestigious artworks and a mausoleum containing graves of the Hohenzollern family. The landscaped gardens are especially lovely in summer, and there are several other noteworthy museums and attractive buildings in the area.

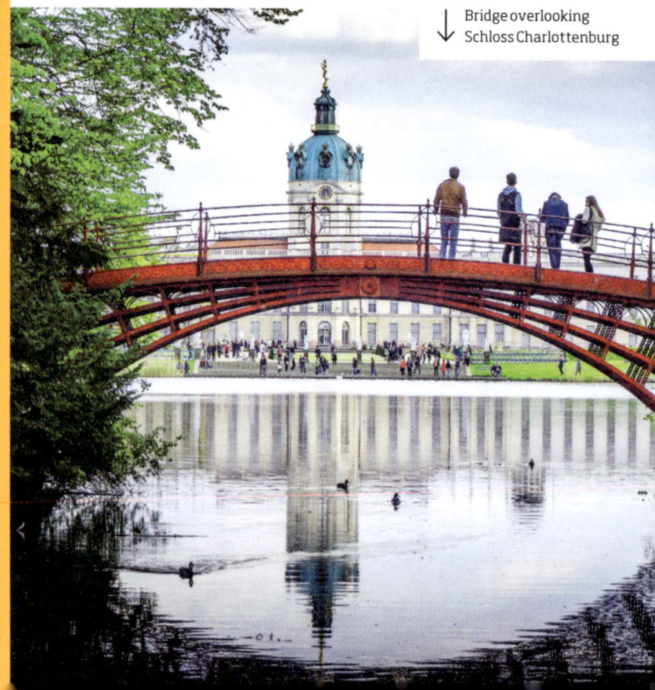

Bridge overlooking Schloss Charlottenburg

SCHLOSS CHARLOTTENBURG

A4 Spandauer Damm 20-24 Jungfernheide, Westend Richard-Wagner-Platz, Sophie-Charlotte-Platz 109, 309, M45 Apr-Oct: 10am-5:30pm Tue-Sun; Nov-Mar: 10am-4:30pm Tue-Sun spsg.de

This opulent Baroque palace was home to the Hohenzollern dynasty. It is made up of two magnificent buildings: the Altes Schloss (Old Palace) and Neuer Flügel (New Wing).

Built in 1695, the palace in Charlottenburg was intended as a summer home for Sophie Charlotte, Friedrich I's wife. Between 1701 and 1713, Johann Friedrich Eosander enlarged the palace, crowning it with a cupola and adding the orangery wing. This section of the palace is now known as the Altes Schloss. The Neuer Flügel extension was undertaken by Frederick the Great (Friedrich II), and designed by Georg Wenzeslaus von Knobelsdorff in the mid-18th century. Restored to its former elegance following World War II, the palace's collection of lavish interiors is unequalled in Berlin.

A statue of the goddess of fortune tops the cupola

INSIDER TIP
Get Festive

The Orangerie was once used as a setting for court festivities in the summer months. Today, it is still a unique events venue, hosting everything from Baroque classical concerts to Christmas dinners.

The Goldene Galerie, a Rococo garden ballroom, dating from 1746

EXPERIENCE MORE

Neuer Pavillon (Schinkel-Pavillon)

B4 Luisenplatz (Schlosspark Charlottenburg) 30 32 09 11 Westend Richard-Wagner-Platz, Sophie-Charlotte-Platz 109, 309, M45 Apr-Oct: 10am-5:30pm Tue-Sun; Nov-Mar: noon-4pm Tue-Sun

This charming Neo-Classical pavilion, with its clean lines and first-floor balcony, was built for Friedrich Wilhelm III and his second wife, Princess Auguste von Liegnitz. During a visit to Naples, the king was so impressed by the Villa Reale del Chiamonte that he commissioned Karl Friedrich Schinkel to build him something similar. The pavilion was finished for the king's birthday on 3 August 1825. Schinkel designed a two-storey structure with a central staircase and ranged the rooms around it in perfect symmetry. Pillared galleries on the first floor added variety to the eastern and western elevations. A cast-iron balcony runs around the entire structure. Like many other Schloss Charlottenburg buildings, the pavilion burned down completely in World War II and was rebuilt in 1960.

The display inside the pavilion reveals the original splendour of the aristocratic interiors, enhanced with pictures and sculptures of the period. The prize picture is a renowned panorama of Berlin dated 1834, painted by Eduard Gärtner from the roof of the Friedrichswerdersche Kirche. You can also admire paintings by Schinkel, not only a great architect but also a fine painter of fabulous architectural fantasies.

Schlosspark

A4 Luisenplatz Westend Richard-Wagner-Platz, Sophie-Charlotte-Platz 109, 309, M45

The extensive palace park that surrounds Schloss Charlottenburg, crisscrossed with tidy gravel paths, is a favourite place for Berliners to stroll at the weekend. The park is largely the result of reconstruction work carried out after World War II, when 18th-century prints were used to help recreate the varied layout of the original grounds.

Immediately behind Schloss Charlottenburg is a French-style Baroque garden, made to a strict geometrical design with a vibrant patchwork of flowerbeds, carefully trimmed shrubs and ornate fountains. Further away from the palace, beyond the curved carp lake, is a less formal English-style landscaped park, originally laid out in the 1820s under the direction of the renowned royal gardener, Peter Joseph Lenné. The lakes and waterways of the park are the habitat of various waterfowl, including herons. A bike path runs along the Spree from the palace park to the Tiergarten and beyond.

Mausoleum

A4 Luisenplatz (Schlosspark Charlottenburg) 32 09 14 46 Westend Richard-Wagner-Platz, Sophie-Charlotte-Platz 109, 309, M45 Apr-Oct: 10am-5:30pm Tue-Sun Nov-Mar

Queen Luise, the beloved first wife of Friedrich Wilhelm III, was laid to rest in this modest, dignified building, set among the trees in Schlosspark. The mausoleum was designed by Karl Friedrich Schinkel, in the style of a Doric portico-fronted temple.

In the original design, the queen's sarcophagus was housed in the crypt while the tombstone (a cenotaph sculpted by Christian Daniel Rauch) stood in the centre of the mausoleum. After the death of Friedrich Wilhelm in 1840, the mausoleum was refurbished, an apse added and the queen's tomb moved to one side, leaving room for her husband's tomb, also designed by Rauch. The second wife of the king, Princess Auguste von Liegnitz, was also buried in the crypt of the mausoleum. Between 1890 and 1894, the tombs of Kaiser Wilhelm I and his wife, Auguste von Sachsen-Weimar, were added to the crypt. Both monuments are the work of Erdmann Encke.

Cherubs striking playful poses in royal Schlosspark

Reiterdenkmal des Grossen Kurfürsten

A4 Luisenplatz Westend Richard-Wagner-Platz, Sophie-Charlotte-Platz 109, 309, M45

The Monument to the Great Elector (Friedrich Wilhelm) is the finest in Berlin and was paid for by his son, Elector Friedrich III (later King Friedrich I). Designed by Andreas Schlüter to be cast in one piece, the statue was completed in 1703, and erected near the former Berlin palace, by Lange Brücke (now called Rathausbrücke). The statue was moved to safety in World War II, but ironically, on the return journey, the barge transporting the monument sank in the port of Tegel.

In 1949 the statue was retrieved intact from the water and erected here on a copy of the base. The original base finally ended up in the Bode-Museum topped with a replica of the statue. The statue portrays the Great Elector on horseback, with the figures of prisoners of war around the base. The base itself is decorated with patriotic reliefs of allegorical scenes. One scene depicts the kingdom surrounded by figures representing Peace, History and the Spree river; another shows it protected by embodiments of Bravery, Faith and Strength (represented by the figure of Hercules).

EAT

Brauhaus Lemke am Schloss

Set right beside the Schloss Charlottenburg, this classic brewhouse makes a convenient spot for post-tour sustenance. The interior is as reassuringly traditional as the menu, which features home-brewed beer and filling, meat-heavy German food.

B4 Luisenplatz Noon-midnight daily lemke.berlin

Käthe-Kollwitz-Museum

A4 Spandauer Damm 10 Westend Richard-Wagner-Platz, Sophie-Charlotte-Platz 109, 309, M45 Hours vary, check website kaethe-kollwitz.de

This museum provides a unique opportunity to become acquainted with the work of Käthe Kollwitz (1867–1945). Born in Königsberg, the artist settled in Berlin, where she married a doctor who worked in Prenzlauer Berg, a working-class district. Her drawings and sculptures portrayed the social problems of the poor, as well as human tragedy and suffering. She frequently took up the theme of motherhood and war after losing a son and grandson in World Wars I and II.

Schlossstrasse Villas

A5 Schlossstrasse 65-67 Sophie-Charlotte-Platz 309

Most of the historic villas and buildings that once graced Schlossstrasse no longer exist. However, careful restoration of a few villas enables the visitor to get a feel for what the atmosphere must have been like at the end of the 19th century. It is worth taking a stroll down Schlossstrasse to look at the renovated villas, especially No. 67, which was built in 1873 in a Neo-Classical style to a design by Georg Töbelmann. If you continue the walk down nearby Schustehrusstrasse, you'll see an interesting school building at No. 39–43. Just up the road at No. 55 is the Villa Oppenheim, home of the Charlottenburg-Wilmersdorf Museum, open to the public except on Mondays.

Did You Know?

Charlottenburg was named after Sophie Charlotte of Hanover after she died in 1705.

Luisenkirche

B5 Gierkeplatz 4 341 90 61 Richard-Wagner-Platz, Sophie-Charlotte-Platz 109, M45 9am-1pm Mon, Tue, Thu & Fri; 2-6pm Wed

This small church dates back to 1716, but its original Baroque styling was removed in rebuilding undertaken by Karl Friedrich Schinkel in the 1820s, when the church was renamed in memory of Queen Luise (1776–1810). The shape of the church is based on a traditional Greek cross, with a tower at the front. The interior fixtures and fittings are not the originals, and the elegant stained-glass windows were made in 1956.

Belvedere

A3 Spandauer Damm 20-4 (Schlosspark Charlottenburg) 32 09 10 Westend Richard-Wagner-Platz, Sophie-Charlotte-Platz 109, 309, M45 Apr-Oct: 10am-5:30pm Tue-Sun Nov-Mar

The Belvedere is a summer house in the Schlosspark which served as a tea pavilion for Friedrich Wilhelm II and, in times of war, as a watchtower. It dates from 1788 and was designed by Carl Gotthard Langhans. The architect mixed Baroque and Neo-Classical elements, giving the building an oval central structure with four straight-sided annexes. The building is crowned by a low dome topped with a sculpture of three cherubs supporting a basket of flowers. Though the Belvedere was ruined during World War II, the summer house was reconstructed between 1956 and 1960 and adapted to serve as an exhibition space. The exhibition is a large collection of exquisite

→

Spiral staircase below the cupola of the Museum Scharf-Gerstenberg

porcelain from the Berlin Königliche Porzellan-Manufaktur (Royal Porcelain Workshop), which has pieces from the Rococo period up to late Biedermeier.

Museum Scharf-Gerstenberg

B4 Schlossstrasse 70 Richard-Wagner-Platz, Sophie-Charlotte-Platz Westend 309, M45 10am-6pm Tue-Fri, 11am-6pm Sat & Sun smb.museum

The two 1850s pavilions on either side of Schlossstrasse were intended as officers' barracks for the King's Guard du Corps. Adjoining the eastern one is the Marstall, or stable block, and in this can be found the Museum Scharf-Gerstenberg. The museum presents paintings, sculptures, works on paper and even films by Surrealist and associated artists such as Dalí, Magritte, Max Ernst, Paul Klee and Jean Dubuffet, and also older works by Goya, Piranesi and Redon. More than 250 objects are presented over three floors, explaining the history of surreal art, with pieces from almost all the leading Surrealists.

Museum Berggruen

A4 Schlossstrasse 1 Westend Richard-Wagner-Platz, Sophie-Charlotte-Platz 109, 309, M45 For renovation smb.museum

Heinz Berggruen assembled this tasteful collection of art dating from the late 19th and first half of the 20th century. Born and educated in Berlin, he emigrated to the US in 1936, spent most of his later life in Paris, but later entrusted his collection to the city of his birth. The museum opened in what was once the west pavilion of the barracks using space freed up by moving the Antikensammlung to Museumsinsel. The exhibition halls were modified according to the designs of Hilmer and Sattler, who also designed the layout of the Gemäldegalerie. The Museum Berggruen is particularly well known for its large collection of quality paintings, drawings and gouaches by Pablo Picasso. The collection begins with a drawing from his student days in 1897 and ends with works he painted in 1972, one year before his death.

In addition to these, the museum displays more than 60 works by Swiss artist Paul Klee and more than 20 works by Henri Matisse. The museum also houses paintings by other major artists, such as Georges Braque and Paul Cézanne.

Bröhan-Museum

A5 Schlossstrasse 1a Westend Richard-Wagner-Platz, Sophie-Charlotte-Platz 109, 309, M45 10am-6pm Tue-Sun broehan-museum.de

This small but interesting museum, set in a late Neo-Classical building, houses a collection of decorative arts amassed by Karl H Bröhan, who from 1966 collected works of art from the Art Nouveau (Jugendstil or Secessionist) and Art Deco periods. The paintings of the artists particularly connected with the Berlin Secessionist movement, such as Karl Hagemeister and Hans Baluschek, are especially well represented. Alongside the paintings there are fine examples of arts and crafts in other media: furniture, ceramics, silverwork and textiles. There is glasswork by Émile Gallé and porcelain from some of the finest European manufacturers.

BEFORE YOU GO

Forward planning is essential to any successful trip. Be prepared for all eventualities by considering the following points before you travel.

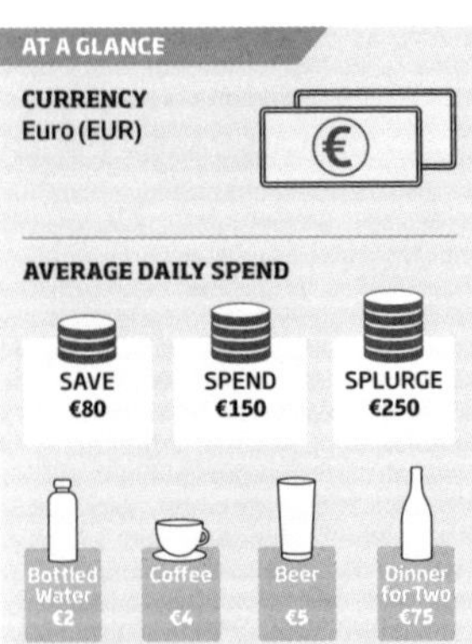

ESSENTIAL PHRASES

Hello	Guten Tag
Goodbye	Auf Wiedersehen
Please	Bitte
Thank you	Danke
Do you speak English?	Sprechen Sie Englisch?
I don't understand	Ich verstehe nicht

ELECTRICITY SUPPLY

Power sockets are type F, fitting two-pronged plugs. Standard voltage is 230 volts.

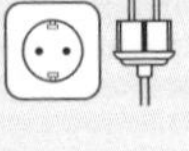

Passports and Visas

For entry requirements, including visas, consult the German embassy or check the **German Federal Foreign Office** website. Citizens of the UK, US, Canada, Australia and New Zealand do not need visas for stays of up to three months but in future must apply in advance for the European Travel Information and Authorization System **(ETIAS)**. Visitors from other countries may also require an ETIAS, so check before travelling. EU nationals do not need a visa or an ETIAS.

German Federal Foreign Office
W auswaertiges-amt.de
European Travel Information and Authorization System (ETIAS)
W travel-europe.europa.eu/etias_en

Government Advice

The **UK Foreign, Commonwealth & Development Office**, the **US Department of State**, the **Australian Department of Foreign Affairs and Trade** and the **German Federal Foreign Office** offer the latest information on security,health and local regulations.

Australian Department of Foreign Affairs and Trade
W smartraveller.gov.au
UK Foreign, Commonwealth & Development Office
W gov.uk/foreign-travel-advice
US Department of State
W travel.state.gov

Customs Information

You can find information on the laws relating to goods and currency taken in or out of Germany from the **Zoll** (Federal Customs Service) website.

Zoll W zoll.de

Insurance

Take out a comprehensive insurance policy covering theft, loss of belongings, medical care, cancellation and delays, and read the small print carefully.

EU citizens are eligible for free emergency medical care in Germany provided they have a valid **EHIC** (European Health Insurance Card) or **GHIC** (UK Global Health Insurance Card)

EHIC
W ec.europa.eu
GHIC
W gov.uk/global-health-insurance-card

Vaccinations

No inoculations are needed for Germany.

Booking Accommodation

Berlin offers a variety of accommodation to suit any budget, ranging from five-star hotels to family-run B&Bs and budget hostels.

Lodgings can fill up during the busy summer months, and prices are inflated during peak season, so book in advance.

A comprehensive list of accommodation to suit all needs can be found on **Visit Berlin**, the city's official tourism website.

Visit Berlin
W visitberlin.de

Money

Major credit, debit and prepaid currency cards are accepted in most shops and chains. Contactless payments have become the norm since the COVID-19 pandemic, though it is still not used on public transport. It is always worth carrying cash, as some smaller businesses don't accept card payments.

Travellers with Specific Requirements

Berlin's wide streets and open spaces make it a wheelchair-friendly city. Pavements are sloped at junctions and most public buildings are fitted with lifts and ramps. Wheelchairs can be hired from the **German Red Cross** (DRK).

Not all S- and U-Bahn stations are equipped with lifts. If you are in the U-Bahn, wait at the head of the platform and the driver will put up a ramp. In the S-Bahn, speak to the station manager to have a ramp set up. BVG maps show all of the accessible stations. Buses with a wheelchair symbol have a ramp. Download the free **accessBerlin** app for details of the most accessible routes around the city.

Berlin's charitable association for the blind and sight-impaired, the **Allgemeiner Blindenund Sehbehindertenverein**, offers practical advice and useful information.

Allgemeiner Blindenund Sehbehindertenverein
W absv.de
DRK
W drk-berlin.de/reservierung.html

Language

German is the official language, but Berlin is an international city, and English is almost as prevalent as German.

Opening Hours

Situations can change quickly and unexpectedly. Always check before visiting attractions and hospitality venues for up-to-date opening hours and booking requirements.

Monday Many museums and some major tourist attractions are closed for the day.

Sunday Most shops and some small businesses close early or for the entire day.

Public holidays Schools, post offices and banks are closed for the entire day.

GETTING AROUND

Once divided between East and West, Berlin is now connected by an excellent public transport system that crisscrosses the city and beyond.

AT A GLANCE

PUBLIC TRANSPORT COSTS
Tickets are valid on all forms of public transport in Berlin.

SINGLE
€3.80
(zones A-B)

DAY TICKET
€9.90
(zones A-B)

7-DAY TICKET
€41.30
(zones A-B)

SPEED LIMIT

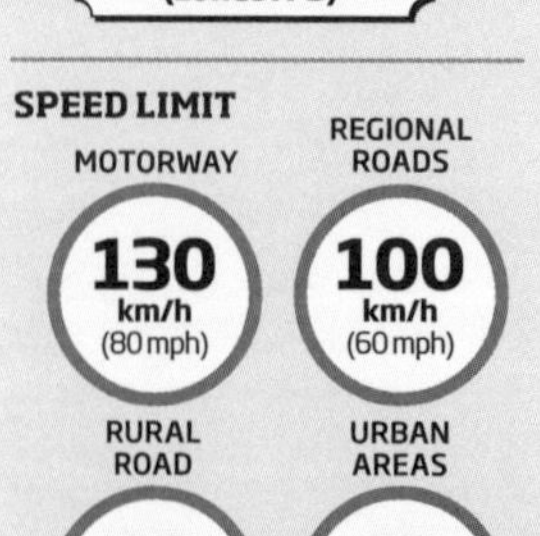

Arriving by Air

Berlin's two international airports, Tegel (TXL) and Schönefeld (SXF), were replaced in October 2020 by a new regional hub, the **Berlin-Brandenburg (BER)**. Situated some 18 km (11 miles) southeast of the city, Berlin-Brandenburg is well connected and receives regular flights from Europe, North America and Asia. Schönefeld now operates as Brandenburg's fifth terminal.

The fastest ways to and from the airport are the S-Bahn lines S9 and S45, the commuter trains RE8, RB22, RB23 and RB14 or the FEX Airport Express, direct to Berlin Hauptbahnhof in 30 minutes. Regular buses link the airport to the U-Bahn network.

BER W berlin-airport.de

International Train Travel

International high-speed trains connect Berlin to other major cities across Europe. Reservations for these services are essential. You can buy tickets and passes for multiple international train journeys from **Eurail** or **Interrail**. You may need to pay an additional reservation fee depending on which service you travel with. Always check that your pass is valid on the service you wish to travel with before boarding. **Eurostar** runs a regular service from London to Brussels via the Channel Tunnel, where you can change for Berlin. **Deutsche Bahn** also runs a regular high-speed service to and from many other European destinations.

Students and those under the age of 26 can benefit from discounted rail travel both to and in Germany. For more information, visit these websites.

Deutsche Bahn W bahn.de
Eurail W eurail.com
Eurostar W eurostar.com
Interrail W interrail.eu

Long-Distance Bus Travel

Eurolines offers many coach routes to Berlin from other European cities. Fares start from £19, with additional discounts for students, children and seniors. Other services include **FlixBus**, **Student Agency Bus** and **Ecolines**.

Berlin's central bus station, the **Zentraler Omnibusbahnhof (ZOB)**, is the city's largest long-distance bus station with connections to other towns and cities all over Germany and throughout the rest of Europe. Check online for the latest timetables and ticket prices.

Ecolines W ecolines.net
Eurolines W eurolines.eu
FlixBus W flixbus.de
Student Agency Bus W studentagencybus.com
ZOB W zob.berlin

Public Transport

The **Berliner Verkehrsbetriebe (BVG)** is Berlin's main public transport authority and service provider. Safety and hygiene measures, timetables, ticket information, transport maps and more can be found online.

BVG W bvg.de

Tickets

Berlin is divided into three zones: A, B and C. Zone A covers the city centre, Zone B the outskirts of town, and Zone C includes Berlin's suburban areas, Potsdam and its environs, as well as Berlin-Brandenburg airport. Tickets are available for each combination of zones and are valid on all forms of public transport, including regional and local trains, S-Bahn, U-Bahn and ferries, for two hours, with unlimited changes.

Ticket machines at train stations and on board trams accept cash only. Newer trains also accept debit cards (German only). Exact change is required on buses. Tickets are validated in the red or yellow time-stamping machine. If caught without a valid ticket you may face a €60 fine. Travel is only valid in one direction, so a second ticket is required for the return journey. Short-trip *(Kurzstrecke)* tickets are cheaper, but can only be used for three stops on trains and six stops on buses and trams. Daily *(Tageskarte)* and seven-day tickets *(7-Tageskarte)*, costing €8.80 and €36 respectively for zones A–B, are much better value for those planning on making multiple journeys. Seven-day tickets also allow you to travel with one extra adult or up to three children for free after 8pm on weekends and public holidays. Discounted tickets are available with some tourist cards that combine public transport with museum entry.

Regional and Local Train Travel

Germany's railways are operated by Deutsche Bahn (DB). The Regional Bahn and Regional Express (RB and RE) trains service the wider Berlin-Brandenburg region and beyond. Use this service for day trips to Potsdam and other smaller towns near Berlin. Tickets can be bought from automatic machines on station platforms or from ticket offices. Special offers include a five-person ticket that is valid for one day. Berlin has a universal ticketing system. This means that tickets for RB and RE services are also valid on the S-Bahn and U-Bahn, as well as on other public transport services in Berlin.

U-Bahn

Don't be confused by the name, Berlin's "underground" trains also run on elevated tracks above ground. There are ten U-Bahn lines in total, each connecting with S-Bahn and other U-Bahn lines at various points across the city. The service usually closes down between 12:30am and 4am. On weekends all lines are open 24 hours except the U4 and U55. U-Bahn stations are marked by a rectangular blue sign, featuring a large, white letter U.

S-Bahn

The S-Bahn is faster than the U-Bahn, and its stations are further apart from one another. Berlin has 16 S-Bahn lines in total, running well beyond the confines of the city. Trains run every 10 or 20 minutes, or more frequently during peak travel times. S-Bahn stations are marked by a round, green sign, featuring a large, white letter S.

Buses

Several bus services operate in Berlin, and conveniently they all use the same ticket tariffs. Regular buses are marked by three-digit route codes and operate every 20 minutes between 5am and midnight. Important routes are serviced by Metro buses (marked by a letter "M" before the route number), operating 24 hours a day, and running every 10 to 20 minutes, whilst express buses (marked by a letter "X") run every 5 to 20 minutes. The night bus service operates every half an hour from midnight until 4am when the U-Bahn service resumes. Regular tickets are not valid on this service. Night bus tickets can be bought directly from the driver (cash only). All bus routes have a detailed timetable on display at each stop, and inner-city bus stops are equipped with digital screens indicating waiting times. Consult the BVG website for specific route information.

Trams

Despite only servicing the eastern parts of the city, trams *(Strassenbahn)* are a popular way to get around for locals and tourists alike, particularly if you are travelling from Mitte to any part of Prenzlauer Berg. Important routes are serviced by Metro trams running every 10 or 20 minutes, 24 hours a day. Some run a reduced service on weekends. Other tram services run every 20 minutes between 5 or 6 am and midnight. Berlin's integrated transport system allows the use of tram tickets on buses, S- and U-Bahn train services, and vice versa. Tickets can be purchased at the usual vending points, or by using machines (coin only) on board.

Taxis

Official Berlin taxis are cream, have a "Taxi" sign on the roof and have a meter on the driver's dashboard. Taxi apps such as Uber and Lyft also operate in Berlin. Also popular is **BVG Mulva**, an on-demand ride sharing service. Taxis can be hailed on the street, picked up at an official taxi rank *(Würfelfunk)*, or booked in advance online or over the phone from firms such as **Taxi Funk Berlin** or **Würfelfunk**. If you are travelling 2 km (1 mile) or less, ask for a short trip *(Kurzstrecke)* for €5 – this can only be done in taxis you have hailed from the street.

BVG Mulva W bvg.de/en/connections/bvg-muva
Taxi Funk Berlin W funk-taxi-berlin.de
Würfelfunk W wuerfelfunk.de

Driving

Driving licences issued by any of the European Union member states are valid throughout the EU. If visiting from outside the EU, you may need to apply for an International Driving Permit. Check with your local automobile association before you travel.

Driving to Berlin

Berlin is connected to other major European cities via E-roads, which form the International European Road Network.

Germany's regional roads *(Landesstrassen)* are marked with yellow road signs, whilst motorways *(Autobahnen)* are marked with blue road signs. Some stretches of motorway have variable speed limits depending on weather and road conditions; others have no enforced speed limit at all. German drivers therefore tend to zoom along at high speeds reaching up to 200 km/h (125 mph). Berlin is surrounded by a circular motorway called the Berliner Ring, which has numerous signposted exits into the city centre. Drivers must carry their passport and insurance documentation with them at all times if driving a foreign-registered vehicle in Germany.

Contact **ADAC Auto Assistance** in the event of a vehicle breakdown, accident or if you need assistance on the road.
ADAC Auto Assistance W adac.de

Car Rental

You must be 21 or over and have held a valid driver's licence for at least a year to rent a car in Germany. By law, drivers aged 21–2 must purchase a Collision Damage Waiver (CDW). Drivers under the age of 25 may incur a young-driver surcharge.

Driving in Berlin

Berlin is relatively straightforward to navigate by car; road layouts are clear and streets are well signposted. Parking is also relatively cheap compared to other major European cities.

If you are flying to Berlin and staying within the metro area, the most efficient way to travel is by public transport. There are also park-and-ride facilities on the outskirts, which are cheaper than inner-city parking.

When driving in the city, beware of cyclists and trams. Trams take precedence; take care when turning; and allow cyclists right of way.

Rules of the Road

Drive on the right. Unless otherwise signposted, vehicles coming from the right have priority.

Drivers must always carry a valid driver's licence, registration and insurance documents. Seatbelts are compulsory in a hired car, lights must be used in tunnels and the use of a mobile phone while driving is prohibited, with the exception of a hands-free system. The drink-drive limit is strictly enforced.

All drivers must have third-party insurance *(Haftpflichtversicherung)* – it is the minimum insurance requirement in Germany. Also compulsory is an environmental badge for vehicles driving within environmental green zones known as **Umweltzonen**. Majority of downtown Berlin is classified as an *Umweltzone*. Certification can be purchased online.

Umweltzonen W umwelt-plakette.de

Cycling

Berlin is generally a bike-friendly city, with many designated cycle lanes and traffic lights at intersections. Should you get tired of pedalling, bicycles can be taken on the U-Bahn, S-Bahn and trams, but they are prohibited on buses, except night buses, which can carry up to two at the driver's discretion.

For all public transport an additional *Fahrrad* (bicycle) ticket is required.

Bicycle Hire

Deutsche Bahn operates an excellent public bicycle system called **Call a Bike**. Bikes can be picked up from train stations and major intersections. They can be dropped off at any of the Call a Bike stations conveniently dotted throughout the city.

To rent a Call a Bike, you must register by providing your credit card details. On the basic tariff, a €1 unlock fee is applied to each ride. The first 15 minutes cost €1 and a maximum fee of €9 is charged per day. Additional fees are applied if bikes are not returned to train stations.

You can also hire bikes at many cycling shops for similar or cheaper rates; one of the most reliable is **Fahrradstation**. Be aware that drink-drive limits also apply to cyclists.

Call a Bike
W callabike.de
Fahrradstation
W fahrradstation.com

Bicycle Safety

Ride on the right. If you are unsure or unsteady, practise in one of the inner-city parks first. If in doubt, dismount and walk with your bicycle: many cyclists prefer to cross busy junctions on foot; if you do so, switch to the pedestrian section of the crossing. Beware of tram tracks; always try to cross them at an angle to avoid getting the bicycle wheels stuck.

For your own safety, do not walk with your bike in a bike lane or cycle on pavements, on the left side of the road, in pedestrian zones or in the dark without lights. The locals usually don't bother, but wearing a helmet is recommended.

PRACTICAL INFORMATION

A little local know-how goes a long way in Berlin. Here you will find all the essential advice and information you will need during your stay.

AT A GLANCE

EMERGENCY NUMBERS

GENERAL EMERGENCY	POLICE
112	110

TIME ZONE
CET/CEST
Central European Summer Time (CEST) is observed Mar-Oct.

TAP WATER
Unless otherwise stated, tap water in Germany is safe to drink.

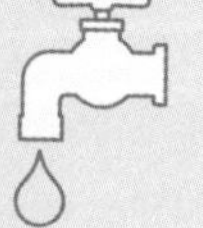

WEBSITES

Visit Berlin
The city's official tourist information website (visitberlin.de)

accessBerlin
A free app detailing the most accessible routes around the city

BVG FahrInfo Plus
Live departures and travel updates from the city's local transport operator BVG

Berlin Wall Art
This free app reconstructs the Iron Curtain with the last and most complete photo collection of the Berlin Wall.

Personal Security

Pickpockets are known to work crowded buses and tourist areas. Contact your embassy if your passport has been stolen, or in the event of a serious crime or accident. Berliners are generally accepting of people of all races, gender or sexuality. Homosexuality was legalized in Germany in 1994. However, acceptance is not always a given. If you do feel unsafe, the **Safe Space Alliance** pinpoints your nearest place of refuge. The **Maneo** emergency hotline run by **Mann-O-Meter** supports victims of homophobic behaviour. **Lesbenberatung** is a lesbian safe space that offers help and counselling for women, girls and transgender people.

Lesbenberatung W esbenberatung-berlin.de
Maneo W maneo.de
Mann-O-Meter W mann-o-meter.de
Safe Space Alliance W safespacealliance.com

Health

Berlin is known for its world-class health service. EU and UK citizens can receive emergency medical treatment free of charge, but you may have to pay upfront and reclaim on your insurance later. For other visitors, payment is the patient's responsibility. It is therefore important to arrange comprehensive medical insurance before travelling. For minor ailments go to a pharmacy *(Apotheke)*. Details of the nearest 24-hour service *(Notdienst)* are posted in all pharmacy windows and on the **Apothekerkammer** website.

Apothekerkammer W akberlin.de

Smoking, Alcohol and Drugs

Germany has a smoking ban in all public places, including bars, cafés, restaurants and hotels. However, many establishments circumvent these laws by naming themselves a *Raucherkneipe*, or smoking pub.

Since 2024, the possession of up to 25 g (0.8 oz) of cannabis is legal for adults but it remains illegal to purchase or sell cannabis. The possession of other narcotics is strictly prohibited and could result in prosecution and a prison sentence.

Unless stated otherwise, it is permitted to drink alcohol on the streets and in public parks and gardens. Germany has a strict limit of 0.05 per cent BAC (blood alcohol content) for drivers.

ID

There is no requirement for visitors to carry ID, but in the event of a routine check you may be asked to show your passport. If you don't have it with you, the police may escort you to wherever your passport is being kept.

Local Customs

Germany has strict laws on hate speech and symbols linked to Adolf Hitler and Nazism. Disrespectful behaviour in public places can warrant a fine, or even lead to prosecution. Be respectful when visiting Berlin's historical sights and monuments. Pay attention to signage indicating when photos aren't allowed.

Visiting Places of Worship

Dress respectfully: cover your torso, upper arms and knees.

Mobile Phones and Wi-Fi

Free Wi-Fi hotspots are widely available in Berlin's city centre. Cafés and restaurants are usually happy to permit the use of their Wi-Fi on the condition that you make a purchase.

Visitors travelling to Berlin with EU tariffs will be able to use their devices abroad without being affected by data roaming charges. This means that you pay the same rates as you would at home.

Post

German post offices and post boxes are usually easy to spot with their distinctive yellow *Deutsche Post* signs.

Stamps *(Briefmarke)* can be bought in post offices, newsagents, tobacconists and most major supermarkets. There are usually self-service stamp machines conveniently placed outside post offices.

Taxes and Refunds

VAT is 19% in Germany. Non-EU residents are entitled to a tax refund subject to certain conditions. In order to do this, you must request a tax receipt and export papers *(Ausfuhrbescheinigung)* when you purchase your goods. When leaving the country, present these papers, along with the receipt and your ID, at customs to receive your refund.

Discount Cards

The **Berlin Welcome Card** offers free entry to 30 major tourist attractions and discounted entry for nearly 200 more. It also includes unlimited use of public transport during your trip.

With the **Berlin Pass**, visitors get free entry to over 60 attractions, tours and museums and the option of an integrated travel card.

Save up to 30% on the city's top 10 tourist attractions and enjoy unlimited free travel on public transport with the **Berlin City Tour Card**.

Berlin City Tour Card
W citytourcard.com
Berlin Pass
W berlinpass.com
Berlin Welcome Card
W berlin-welcomecard.de

INDEX

ACKNOWLEDGMENTS

Dorling Kindersley would like to extend special thanks to the following people for their contribution: Anamika Bhandari, Syed Mohammad Farhan, Shikha Kulkarni, Narender Kumar, Robin Moul, Shanker Prasad, Rohit Rojal, Priyanka Thakur.

The publisher would like to thank the following for their kind permission to reproduce their photographs:

Key: a-above; b-below/bottom; c-centre; f-far; l-left; r-right; t-top

123RF.com: iloveotto 62-3t; Lauradibias 58b; T.W. van Urk 92tl. **Alamy Stock Photo:** Berlin-Zeitgeist 81cra; Walter Bibikow 43cr; Eden Breitz 55; Adam Eastland 24-25, 66, 81t; Adam Eastland Art + Architecture 45tl; Scott Goodno 35tc; Manfred Gottschalk 64; Andrew Hasson 85; Peter Horree 45cr; Image Professionals GmbH / Spörl, Lukas 90; Iain Masterton 69br, 82tl, 89tl; mauritius images GmbH / Torsten Elger 40br; Miva Stock / DanitaDelimont 97tr; Prisma Archivo 24cr; Lothar Steiner 28; StockFood GmbH / Inga Wandinger 101bl; travelpix 61tl; travelstock44.de / Juergen Held 80b; Tetiana Tuchyk 86; Martin Weiser / CTK 71; Urbanmyth 78-79; Julie g Woodhouse 7tr, 67bl. **AWL Images:** Sabine Lubenow 3tl. **Berliner Ensemble:** Lovis Ostenrick 48br. **C/O Berlin:** 94br. **Depositphotos Inc:** Konrad Kerker 96b. **Dorling Kindersley:** Dorota and Mariusz Jarymowicz 47tr, 50bc. **Dreamstime.com:** 22tomtom 34bl; Andersastphoto 13br; Anticiclo 37tr; Boris Breytman 35tr; Andrea Calistri 20b; Carolannefreeling 36b; Claudiodivizia 44-45b; Eddygaleotti 16-17; Alexandre Fagundes De Fagundes 21t; Alessandro Flore 23br; Gekaskr 6b; Hanohiki 76; Ixuskmitl 33cra; Katatonia82 70bl, 98br; Markwaters 57tl, 60cb; Meinzahn 42b; Mijeshots 8t; Minnystock 2t, 74-5b; Jaroslav Moravcik 23cr; Rumifaz 10bl; Jozef Sedmak 35crb; Tomas1111 26, 38tr; Tupungato 54t; Yorgy67 97crb. **Festival of Lights:** Frank Hermann 23tr. **Getty Images:** Jon Arnold 4-5b; matthewleesdixon 65; mije_shots 32; Moment Open / Federica Gentile 59tl; Nikada 18-19. **Getty Images / iStock:** Giflishtih 56br; holgs 91bl; kavunchik 12tr; Maxlevoyou 88bl; Nikada 51tl; querbeet 30tl; Ziutograf 24bl. **Robert Harding Picture Library:** Stefan Huwiler 15br. **Sammlung Boros:** Installationsansicht mit Arbeiten von Michel Majerus / © NOSHE 49tl. **Shutterstock.com:** Pani Garmyder 52. **Staatliche Museen Zu Berlin:** David von Becker 21cr. © **Stadtmuseum Berlin:** Foto Setzpfandt 39bl. **Urban Nation Museum for Urban Contemporary Art:** Sabine Dobre 72tr. **Zeughaus (Deutsches Historisches Museum):** Thomas Bruns 7tl.

PHRASE BOOK

IN AN EMERGENCY

Where is the telephone?	**Wo ist das telefon?**	*voh ist duss tele-fon?*
Help!	**Hilfe!**	**hilf**-*uh*
Please call a doctor	**Bitte rufen Sie einen Arzt**	**bitt**-*uh* **roof**'*n zee ine-en artst*
Please call the police	**Bitte rufen Sie die Polizei**	**bitt**-*uh* **roof**'*n zee dee poli*-**tsy**
Please call the fire brigade	**Bitte rufen Sie die Feuerwehr**	**bitt**-*uh roof'n zee dee* **foyer**-*vayr*
Stop!	**Halt!**	**hult**

COMMUNICATION ESSENTIALS

Yes	**Ja**	**yah**
No	**Nein**	**nine**
Please	**Bitte**	**bitt**-*uh*
Thank you	**Danke**	*dunk-uh*
Excuse me	**Verzeihung**	*fair*-**tsy**-*hoong*
Hello (good day)	**Guten Tag**	**goot**-*en tahk*
Goodbye	**Auf Wiedersehen**	*owf*-**veed**-*er-zay-ern*
What is that?	**Was ist das?**	*voss ist duss*
Why?	**Warum?**	*var*-**room**
Where?	**Wo?**	**voh**
When?	**Wann?**	**vunn**
today	**heute**	**hoyt**-*uh*
tomorrow	**morgen**	**morg**'*n*
month	**Monat**	**mohn**-*aht*
night	**Nacht**	**nukht**
afternoon	**Nachmittag**	**nahkh**-*mit-tahk*
morning	**Morgen**	**morg**'*n*
year	**Jahr**	*yar*
there	**dort**	**dort**
here	**hier**	**hear**
week	**Woche**	**vokh**-*uh*
yesterday	**gestern**	**gest**'*n*

USEFUL PHRASES

How are you? (informal)	**Wie geht's?**	*vee gayts*
Fine, thanks	**Danke, es geht mir gut**	*dunk-uh, es gayt meer goot*
Until later	**Bis später**	*biss* **shpay**-*ter*
Where is/are?	**Wo ist/ sind...?**	*voh ist/sind*
How far is it to...?	**Wie weit ist es...?**	*vee* **vite** *ist ess*
Do you speak English?	**Sprechen Sie Englisch?**	*shpresh'n zee* **eng**-*glish*
I don't understand	**Ich verstehe nicht**	*ish fair*-**shtay**-*uh nisht*
Could you speak more slowly?	**Könnten Sie langsamer sprechen?**	**kurnt**-*en zee* **lung**-*zam-er* **shpresh**'*n*

USEFUL WORDS

large	**gross**	**grohss**
small	**klein**	**kline**
hot	**heiss**	**hyce**
cold	**kalt**	**kult**
good	**gut**	**goot**
bad	**böse/ schlecht**	**burss**-*uh/* **shlesht**
open	**geöffnet**	*g'***urff**-*nett*
closed	**geschlossen**	*g'***shloss**'*n*
left	**links**	**links**
right	**rechts**	**reshts**
straight ahead	**geradeaus**	*g'***rah**-*der*-**owss**

SHOPPING

Do you have/ Is there...?	**Gibt es...?**	*geept ess*
How much does it cost?	**Was kostet das?**	*voss* **kost**'*t duss?*
When do you open/ close?	**Wann öffnen Sie? schliessen Sie?**	*vunn* **off**'*n zee* **shlees**'*n zee*
this	**das**	*duss*
expensive	**teuer**	**toy**-*er*
cheap	**preiswert**	**price**-*vurt*
size	**Grösse**	**gruhs**-*uh*
number	**Nummer**	**noom**-*er*
colour	**Farbe**	**farb**-*uh*
brown	**braun**	*brown*
black	**schwarz**	**shvarts**
red	**rot**	**roht**
blue	**blau**	**blau**
green	**grün**	**groon**
yellow	**gelb**	**gelp**